SELECTED POEMS

of

LANGSTON HUGHES

SELECTED POEMS

POEMS

of

LANGSTON HUGHES

VINTAGE BOOKS
A Division of Random House, New York

VINTAGE BOOKS EDITION, May 1974
Copyright © 1959 by Langston Hughes. All rights reserved
under International and Pan-American Copyright Conven-
tions. Published in the United States by Random House,
Inc., New York, and simultaneously in Canada by Random
House of Canada, Limited, Toronto. Originally published
by Alfred A. Knopf, Inc., in 1959.

Library of Congress Cataloging in Publication Data

Hughes, Langston, 1902–1967.
  Selected poems of Langston Hughes.

  I. Title.
[PS3515.U274A6   1974]   811'.5'2   73–14913
ISBN 0–394–71910–7
Manufactured in the United States of America
89B

TO MY COUSIN, FLORA

This book contains a selection
of the poems of Langston Hughes chosen by himself
from his earlier volumes:

THE WEARY BLUES

FINE CLOTHES TO THE JEW

SHAKESPEARE IN HARLEM

FIELDS OF WONDER

ONE-WAY TICKET

MONTAGE OF A DREAM DEFERRED

and from the privately printed limited edition

DEAR LOVELY DEATH

together with a number of new poems published
here for the first time in book form,
some never before anywhere.

CONTENTS

Afro-American Fragments

Feet of Jesus

Shadow of the Blues

Sea and Land

Distance Nowhere

After Hours

Life Is Fine

🚩

Lament over Love

🚩

Magnolia Flowers

🚩

Name in Uphill Letters

🚩

~Madam to You

– Montage of a Dream Deferred

Words Like Freedom

Afro-American Fragments

Afro-American Fragment

So long,
So far away
Is Africa.
Not even memories alive
Save those that history books create,
Save those that songs
Beat back into the blood—
Beat out of blood with words sad-sung
In strange un-Negro tongue—
So long,
So far away
Is Africa.

Subdued and time-lost
Are the drums—and yet
Through some vast mist of race
There comes this song
I do not understand,
This song of atavistic land,
Of bitter yearnings lost
Without a place—
So long,
So far away
Is Africa's
Dark face.

The Negro Speaks of Rivers

I've known rivers:
I've known rivers ancient as the world and older than the
     flow of human blood in human veins.

My soul has grown deep like the rivers.

I bathed in the Euphrates when dawns were young.
I built my hut near the Congo and it lulled me to sleep.
I looked upon the Nile and raised the pyramids above it.
I heard the singing of the Mississippi when Abe Lincoln
     went down to New Orleans, and I've seen its muddy
     bosom turn all golden in the sunset.

I've known rivers:
Ancient, dusky rivers.

My soul has grown deep like the rivers.

Sun Song

Sun and softness,
Sun and the beaten hardness of the earth,
Sun and the song of all the sun-stars
Gathered together—
Dark ones of Africa,
I bring you my songs
To sing on the Georgia roads.

Aunt Sue's Stories

Aunt Sue has a head full of stories.
Aunt Sue has a whole heart full of stories.
Summer nights on the front porch
Aunt Sue cuddles a brown-faced child to her bosom
And tells him stories.

Black slaves
Working in the hot sun,
And black slaves
Walking in the dewy night,
And black slaves
Singing sorrow songs on the banks of a mighty river
Mingle themselves softly
In the flow of old Aunt Sue's voice,
Mingle themselves softly
In the dark shadows that cross and recross
Aunt Sue's stories.

And the dark-faced child, listening,
Knows that Aunt Sue's stories are real stories.
He knows that Aunt Sue never got her stories
Out of any book at all,
But that they came
Right out of her own life.

The dark-faced child is quiet
Of a summer night
Listening to Aunt Sue's stories.

Danse Africaine

The low beating of the tom-toms,
The slow beating of the tom-toms,
  Low . . . slow
  Slow . . . low—
  Stirs your blood.
   Dance!
A night-veiled girl
  Whirls softly into a
  Circle of light.
  Whirls softly . . . slowly,
Like a wisp of smoke around the fire—
  And the tom-toms beat,
  And the tom-toms beat,
And the low beating of the tom-toms
  Stirs your blood.

Negro

I am a Negro:
>Black as the night is black,
>Black like the depths of my Africa.

I've been a slave:
>Caesar told me to keep his door-steps clean.
>I brushed the boots of Washington.

I've been a worker:
>Under my hand the pyramids arose.
>I made mortar for the Woolworth Building.

I've been a singer:
>All the way from Africa to Georgia
>I carried my sorrow songs.
>I made ragtime.

I've been a victim:
>The Belgians cut off my hands in the Congo.
>They lynch me still in Mississippi.

I am a Negro:
>Black as the night is black,
>Black like the depths of my Africa.

American Heartbreak

I am the American heartbreak—
Rock on which Freedom
Stumps its toe—
The great mistake
That Jamestown
Made long ago.

October 16

Perhaps
You will remember
John Brown.

John Brown
Who took his gun,
Took twenty-one companions
White and black,
Went to shoot your way to freedom
Where two rivers meet
And the hills of the
North
And the hills of the
South
Look slow at one another—
And died
For your sake.

Now that you are
Many years free,
And the echo of the Civil War
Has passed away,
And Brown himself
Has long been tried at law,
Hanged by the neck,
And buried in the ground—
Since Harpers Ferry
Is alive with ghosts today,
Immortal raiders
Come again to town—

Perhaps
You will recall
John Brown.

As I Grew Older

It was a long time ago.
I have almost forgotten my dream.
But it was there then,
In front of me,
Bright like a sun—
My dream.

And then the wall rose,
Rose slowly,
Slowly,
Between me and my dream.
Rose slowly, slowly,
Dimming,
Hiding,
The light of my dream.
Rose until it touched the sky—
The wall.

Shadow.
I am black.

I lie down in the shadow.
No longer the light of my dream before me,
Above me.
Only the thick wall.
Only the shadow.

My hands!
My dark hands!
Break through the wall!
Find my dream!
Help me to shatter this darkness,
To smash this night,

To break this shadow
Into a thousand lights of sun,
Into a thousand whirling dreams
Of sun!

My People

The night is beautiful,
So the faces of my people.

The stars are beautiful,
So the eyes of my people.

Beautiful, also, is the sun.
Beautiful, also, are the souls of my people.

Dream Variations

To fling my arms wide
In some place of the sun,
To whirl and to dance
Till the white day is done.
Then rest at cool evening
Beneath a tall tree
While night comes on gently,
    Dark like me—
That is my dream!

To fling my arms wide
In the face of the sun,
Dance! Whirl! Whirl!
Till the quick day is done.
Rest at pale evening . . .
A tall, slim tree . . .
Night coming tenderly
    Black like me.

Feet *of* Jesus

Feet o' Jesus

At the feet o' Jesus,
Sorrow like a sea.
Lordy, let yo' mercy
Come driftin' down on me.

At the feet o' Jesus
At yo' feet I stand.
O, ma little Jesus,
Please reach out yo' hand.

Prayer

I ask you this:
Which way to go?
I ask you this:
Which sin to bear?
Which crown to put
Upon my hair?
I do not know,
Lord God,
I do not know.

Shout

Listen to yo' prophets,
Little Jesus!
Listen to yo' saints!

Fire

Fire,
Fire, Lord!
Fire gonna burn ma soul!

I ain't been good,
I ain't been clean—
I been stinkin', low-down, mean.

Fire,
Fire, Lord!
Fire gonna burn ma soul!

Tell me, brother,
Do you believe
If you wanta go to heaben
Got to moan an' grieve?

Fire,
Fire, Lord!
Fire gonna burn ma soul!

I been stealin',
Been tellin' lies,
Had more women
Than Pharaoh had wives.

Fire,
Fire, Lord!
Fire gonna burn ma soul!
I means Fire, Lord!
Fire gonna burn ma soul!

Sunday Morning Prophecy

*An old Negro minister concludes his sermon in his loudest voice,
having previously pointed out the sins of this world:*

> . . . and now
> When the rumble of death
> Rushes down the drain
> Pipe of eternity,
> And hell breaks out
> Into a thousand smiles,
> And the devil licks his chops
> Preparing to feast on life,
> And all the little devils
> Get out their bibs
> To devour the corrupt bones
> Of this world—
> Oh-ooo-oo-o!
> Then my friends!
> Oh, then! Oh, then!
> What will you do?
>
> You will turn back
> And look toward the mountains.
> You will turn back
> And grasp for a straw.
> You will holler,
> *Lord-d-d-d-d-ah!*
> *Save me, Lord!*
> *Save me!*
> And the Lord will say,
> *In the days of your greatness*
> *I did not hear your voice!*
> The Lord will say,
> *In the days of your richness*

I did not see your face!
The Lord will say,
No-oooo-ooo-oo-o!
I will not save you now!

And your soul
Will be lost!

Come into the church this morning,
Brothers and Sisters,
And be saved—
And give freely
In the collection basket
That I who am thy shepherd
Might live.

Amen!

Sinner

Have mercy, Lord!

Po' an' black
An' humble an' lonesome
An' a sinner in yo' sight.

Have mercy, Lord!

Litany

Gather up
In the arms of your pity
The sick, the depraved,
The desperate, the tired,
All the scum
Of our weary city
Gather up
In the arms of your pity.
Gather up
In the arms of your love—
Those who expect
No love from above.

Angels Wings

The angels wings is white as snow,
  O, white as snow,
   White
    as
     snow.
The angels wings is white as snow,
  But I drug ma wings
  In the dirty mire.
  O, I drug ma wings
  All through the fire.
But the angels wings is white as snow,
  White
   as
    snow.

Judgment Day

They put ma body in the ground,
Ma soul went flyin' o' the town,

Went flyin' to the stars an' moon
A-shoutin', God, I's comin' soon.

O Jesus!

Lord in heaven,
Crown on His head,
Says don't be 'fraid
Cause you ain't dead.

Kind Jesus!

An' now I'm settin' clean an' bright
In the sweet o' ma Lord's sight—
    Clean an' bright,
        Clean an' bright.

Prayer Meeting

Glory! Hallelujah!
The dawn's a-comin'!
Glory! Hallelujah!
The dawn's a-comin'!
A black old woman croons
In the amen-corner of the
Ebecaneezer Baptist Church.
A black old woman croons—
The dawn's a-comin'!

Spirituals

Rocks and the firm roots of trees.
The rising shafts of mountains.
Something strong to put my hands on.

Sing, O Lord Jesus!
Song is a strong thing.
I heard my mother singing
When life hurt her:

Gonna ride in my chariot some day!

The branches rise
From the firm roots of trees.
The mountains rise
From the solid lap of earth.
The waves rise
From the dead weight of sea.

Sing, O black mother!
Song is a strong thing.

Tambourines

Tambourines!
Tambourines!
Tambourines
To the glory of God!
Tambourines
To glory!

A gospel shout
And a gospel song:
Life is short
But God is long!

Tambourines!
Tambourines!
Tambourines
To glory!

Shadow *of the* Blues

The Weary Blues

Droning a drowsy syncopated tune,
Rocking back and forth to a mellow croon,
    I heard a Negro play.
Down on Lenox Avenue the other night
By the pale dull pallor of an old gas light
    He did a lazy sway. . . .
    He did a lazy sway. . . .
To the tune o' those Weary Blues.
With his ebony hands on each ivory key
He made that poor piano moan with melody.
    O Blues!
Swaying to and fro on his rickety stool
He played that sad raggy tune like a musical fool.
    Sweet Blues!
Coming from a black man's soul.
    O Blues!
In a deep song voice with a melancholy tone
I heard that Negro sing, that old piano moan—
    "Ain't got nobody in all this world,
    Ain't got nobody but ma self.
    I's gwine to quit ma frownin'
    And put ma troubles on the shelf."
Thump, thump, thump, went his foot on the floor.
He played a few chords then he sang some more—
    "I got the Weary Blues
    And I can't be satisfied.
    Got the Weary Blues
    And can't be satisfied—
    I ain't happy no mo'
    And I wish that I had died."
And far into the night he crooned that tune.

The stars went out and so did the moon.
The singer stopped playing and went to bed
While the Weary Blues echoed through his head.
He slept like a rock or a man that's dead.

Hope

Sometimes when I'm lonely,
Don't know why,
Keep thinkin' I won't be lonely
By and by.

Late Last Night

Late last night I
Set on my steps and cried.
Wasn't nobody gone,
Neither had nobody died.

I was cryin'
Cause you broke my heart in two.
You looked at me cross-eyed
And broke my heart in two—

So I was cryin'
On account of
You!

Bad Morning

Here I sit
With my shoes mismated.
Lawdy-mercy!
I's frustrated!

Sylvester's Dying Bed

I woke up this mornin'
'Bout half-past three.
All the womens in town
Was gathered round me.

Sweet gals was a-moanin',
"Sylvester's gonna die!"
And a hundred pretty mamas
Bowed their heads to cry.

I woke up little later
'Bout half-past fo',
The doctor 'n' undertaker's
Both at ma do'.

Black gals was a-beggin',
"You can't leave us here!"
Brown-skins cryin', "Daddy!
Honey! Baby! Don't go, dear!"

But I felt ma time's a-comin',
And I know'd I's dyin' fast.
I seed the River Jerden
A-creepin' muddy past—
But I's still Sweet Papa 'Vester,
Yes, sir! Long as life do last!

So I hollers, "Com'ere, babies,
Fo' to love yo' daddy right!"
And I reaches up to hug 'em—
When the Lawd put out the light.

Then everything was darkness
In a great . . . big . . . night.

Wake

Tell all my mourners
To mourn in red—
Cause there ain't no sense
In my bein' dead.

Could Be

Could be Hastings Street,
Or Lenox Avenue,
Could be 18th & Vine
And still be true.

Could be 5th & Mound,
Could be Rampart:
When you pawned my watch
You pawned my heart.

Could be you love me,
Could be that you don't.
Might be that you'll come back,
Like as not you won't.

Hastings Street is weary,
Also Lenox Avenue.
Any place is dreary
Without my watch and you.

Bad Luck Card

Cause you don't love me
Is awful, awful hard.
Gypsy done showed me
My bad luck card.

There ain't no good left
In this world for me.
Gypsy done tole me—
Unlucky as can be.

I don't know what
Po' weary me can do.
Gypsy says I'd kill my self
If I was you.

Reverie on the Harlem River

Did you ever go down to the river—
Two a.m. midnight by your self?
Sit down by the river
And wonder what you got left?

Did you ever think about your mother?
God bless her, dead and gone!
Did you ever think about your sweetheart
And wish she'd never been born?

Down on the Harlem River:
    Two a.m.
    Midnight!
    By your self!
Lawd, I wish I could die—
But who would miss me if I left?

Morning After

I was so sick last night I
Didn't hardly know my mind.
So sick last night I
Didn't know my mind.
I drunk some bad licker that
Almost made me blind.

Had a dream last night I
Thought I was in hell.
I drempt last night I
Thought I was in hell.
Woke up and looked around me—
Babe, your mouth was open like a well.

I said, Baby! Baby!
Please don't snore so loud.
Baby! Please!
Please don't snore so loud.
You jest a little bit o' woman but you
Sound like a great big crowd.

Early Evening Quarrel

Where is that sugar, Hammond,
I sent you this morning to buy?
I say, where is that sugar
I sent you this morning to buy?
Coffee without sugar
Makes a good woman cry.

> *I ain't got no sugar, Hattie,*
> *I gambled your dime away.*
> *Ain't got no sugar, I*
> *Done gambled that dime away.*
> *If you's a wise woman, Hattie,*
> *You ain't gonna have nothin to say.*

I ain't no wise woman, Hammond.
I am evil and mad.
Ain't no sense in a good woman
Bein treated so bad.

> *I don't treat you bad, Hattie,*
> *Neither does I treat you good.*
> *But I reckon I could treat you*
> *Worser if I would.*

Lawd, these things we women
Have to stand!
I wonder is there nowhere a
Do-right man?

Evil

Looks like what drives me crazy
Don't have no effect on you—
But I'm gonna keep on at it
Till it drives you crazy, too.

As Befits a Man

I don't mind dying—
But I'd hate to die all alone!
I want a dozen pretty women
To holler, cry, and moan.

I don't mind dying
But I want my funeral to be fine:
A row of long tall mamas
Fainting, fanning, and crying.

I want a fish-tail hearse
And sixteen fish-tail cars,
A big brass band
And a whole truck load of flowers.

When they let me down,
Down into the clay,
I want the women to holler:
Please don't take him away!
      Ow-ooo-oo-o!
Don't take daddy away!

Sea *and* Land

Havana Dreams

The dream is a cocktail at Sloppy Joe's—
(Maybe—nobody knows.)

The dream is the road to Batabano.
(But nobody knows if that is so.)

Perhaps the dream is only her face—
Perhaps it's a fan of silver lace—
Or maybe the dream's a Vedado rose—
(*Quien sabe?* Who really knows?)

Catch

Big Boy came
Carrying a mermaid
On his shoulders
And the mermaid
Had her tail
Curved
Beneath his arm.

Being a fisher boy,
He'd found a fish
To carry—
Half fish,
Half girl
To marry.

Water-Front Streets

The spring is not so beautiful there—
    But dream ships sail away
To where the spring is wondrous rare
    And life is gay.

The spring is not so beautiful there—
    But lads put out to sea
Who carry beauties in their hearts
    And dreams, like me.

Long Trip

The sea is a wilderness of waves,
A desert of water.
We dip and dive,
Rise and roll,
Hide and are hidden
On the sea.
     Day, night,
     Night, day,
The sea is a desert of waves,
A wilderness of water.

Seascape

Off the coast of Ireland
    As our ship passed by
We saw a line of fishing ships
    Etched against the sky.

Off the coast of England
    As we rode the foam
We saw an Indian merchantman
    Coming home.

Moonlight Night: Carmel

Tonight the waves march
In long ranks
Cutting the darkness
With their silver shanks,
Cutting the darkness
And kissing the moon
And beating the land's
Edge into a swoon.

Heaven

Heaven is
The place where
Happiness is
Everywhere.

Animals
And birds sing—
As does
Everything.

To each stone,
"How-do-you-do?"
Stone answers back,
"Well! And you?"

In Time of Silver Rain

In time of silver rain
The earth
Puts forth new life again,
Green grasses grow
And flowers lift their heads,
And over all the plain
The wonder spreads
      Of life,
      Of life,
      Of life!

In time of silver rain
The butterflies
Lift silken wings
To catch a rainbow cry,
And trees put forth
New leaves to sing
In joy beneath the sky
As down the roadway
Passing boys and girls
Go singing, too,
In time of silver rain
      When spring
      And life
      Are new.

Joy

I went to look for Joy,
Slim, dancing Joy,
Gay, laughing Joy,
Bright-eyed Joy—
And I found her
Driving the butcher's cart
In the arms of the butcher boy!
Such company, such company,
As keeps this young nymph, Joy!

Winter Moon

How thin and sharp is the moon tonight!
How thin and sharp and ghostly white
Is the slim curved crook of the moon tonight!

Snail

Little snail,
Dreaming you go.
Weather and rose
Is all you know.

Weather and rose
Is all you see,
Drinking
The dewdrop's
Mystery.

March Moon

The moon is naked.
The wind has undressed the moon.
The wind has blown all the cloud-garments
Off the body of the moon
And now she's naked,
Stark naked.

But why don't you blush,
O shameless moon?
Don't you know
It isn't nice to be naked?

Harlem Night Song

Come,
Let us roam the night together
Singing.

I love you.

Across
The Harlem roof-tops
Moon is shining.
Night sky is blue.
Stars are great drops
Of golden dew.

Down the street
A band is playing.

I love you.

Come,
Let us roam the night together
Singing.

To Artina

I will take your heart.
I will take your soul out of your body
As though I were God.
I will not be satisfied
With the little words you say to me.
I will not be satisfied
With the touch of your hand
Nor the sweet of your lips alone.
I will take your heart for mine.
I will take your soul.
I will be God when it comes to you.

Fulfilment

The earth-meaning
Like the sky-meaning
Was fulfilled.

We got up
And went to the river,
Touched silver water,
Laughed and bathed
In the sunshine.

Day
Became a bright ball of light
For us to play with,
Sunset
A yellow curtain,
Night
A velvet screen.

The moon,
Like an old grandmother,
Blessed us with a kiss
And sleep
Took us both in
Laughing.

Gypsy Melodies

Songs that break
And scatter
Out of the moon:
Rockets of joy
Dimmed too soon.

Mexican Market Woman

This ancient hag
Who sits upon the ground
Selling her scanty wares
Day in, day round,
Has known high wind-swept mountains,
And the sun has made
Her skin so brown.

A Black Pierrot

I am a black Pierrot:
    She did not love me,
    So I crept away into the night
    And the night was black, too.

I am a black Pierrot:
    She did not love me,
    So I wept until the dawn
    Dripped blood over the eastern hills
    And my heart was bleeding, too.

I am a black Pierrot:
    She did not love me,
    So with my once gay-colored soul
    Shrunken like a balloon without air,
    I went forth in the morning
    To seek a new brown love.

Ardella

I would liken you
To a night without stars
Were it not for your eyes.
I would liken you
To a sleep without dreams
Were it not for your songs.

When Sue Wears Red

When Susanna Jones wears red
Her face is like an ancient cameo
Turned brown by the ages.

Come with a blast of trumpets,
    Jesus!

When Susanna Jones wears red
A queen from some time-dead Egyptian night
Walks once again.

Blow trumpets, Jesus!

And the beauty of Susanna Jones in red
Burns in my heart a love-fire sharp like pain.

Sweet silver trumpets,
    Jesus!

Love

Love is a wild wonder
And stars that sing,
Rocks that burst asunder
And mountains that take wing.

John Henry with his hammer
Makes a little spark.
That little spark is love
Dying in the dark.

Beale Street

The dream is vague
And all confused
With dice and women
And jazz and booze.

The dream is vague,
Without a name,
Yet warm and wavering
And sharp as flame.

The loss
Of the dream
Leaves nothing
The same.

Port Town

Hello, sailor boy,
In from the sea!
Hello, sailor,
Come with me!

Come on drink cognac.
Rather have wine?
Come here, I love you.
Come and be mine.

Lights, sailor boy,
Warm, white lights.
Solid land, kid.
Wild, white nights.

Come on, sailor,
Out o' the sea.
Let's go, sweetie!
Come with me.

Natcha

Natcha, offering love.
For ten shillings offering love.
Offering: A night with me, honey.
A long, sweet night with me.
    Come, drink palm wine.
    Come, drink kisses.
A long, dream night with me.

Young Sailor

He carries
His own strength
And his own laughter,
His own today
And his own hereafter—
This strong young sailor
Of the wide seas.

What is money for?
To spend, he says.
And wine?
To drink.
And women?
To love.
And today?
For joy.
And the green sea
For strength,
And the brown land
For laughter.

And nothing hereafter.

Sea Calm

How still,
How strangely still
The water is today.
It is not good
For water
To be so still that way.

Dream Dust

Gather out of star-dust
>Earth-dust,
>Cloud-dust,
>Storm-dust,

And splinters of hail,
One handful of dream-dust
>Not for sale.

No Regrets

Out of love,
No regrets—
Though the goodness
Be wasted forever.

Out of love,
No regrets—
Though the return
Be never.

Troubled Woman

She stands
In the quiet darkness,
This troubled woman
Bowed by
Weariness and pain
Like an
Autumn flower
In the frozen rain,
Like a
Wind-blown autumn flower
That never lifts its head
Again.

Island

Wave of sorrow,
Do not drown me now:

I see the island
Still ahead somehow.

I see the island
And its sands are fair:

Wave of sorrow,
Take me there.

Distance Nowhere

Border Line

I used to wonder
About living and dying—
I think the difference lies
Between tears and crying.

I used to wonder
About here and there—
I think the distance
Is nowhere.

Garden

Strange
Distorted blades of grass,
Strange
Distorted trees,
Strange
Distorted tulips
On their knees.

Genius Child

This is a song for the genius child.
Sing it softly, for the song is wild.
Sing it softly as ever you can—
Lest the song get out of hand.

Nobody loves a genius child.

Can you love an eagle,
Tame or wild?

Wild or tame,
Can you love a monster
Of frightening name?

Nobody loves a genius child.

Kill him—and let his soul run wild!

Strange Hurt

In times of stormy weather
She felt queer pain
That said,
"You'll find rain better
Than shelter from the rain."

Days filled with fiery sunshine
Strange hurt she knew
That made
Her seek the burning sunlight
Rather than the shade.

In months of snowy winter
When cozy houses hold,
She'd break down doors
To wander naked
In the cold.

Suicide's Note

The calm,
Cool face of the river
Asked me for a kiss.

End

There are
No clocks on the wall,
And no time,
No shadows that move
From dawn to dusk
Across the floor.

There is neither light
Nor dark
Outside the door.

There is no door!

Drum

Bear in mind
That death is a drum
Beating forever
Till the last worms come
To answer its call,
Till the last stars fall,
Until the last atom
Is no atom at all,
Until time is lost
And there is no air
And space itself
Is nothing nowhere,
Death is a drum,
A signal drum,
Calling life
To come!
Come!
Come!

Personal

In an envelope marked:
    Personal
God addressed me a letter.
In an envelope marked:
    Personal
I have given my answer.

Juliet

Wonder
And pain
And terror,
And sick silly songs
Of sorrow,
And the marrow
Of the bone
Of life
Are smeared across
Her mouth.

The road
From Verona
To Mantova
Is dusty
With the drought.

Desire

Desire to us
Was like a double death,
Swift dying
Of our mingled breath,
Evaporation
Of an unknown strange perfume
Between us quickly
In a naked
Room.

Vagabonds

We are the desperate
Who do not care,
The hungry
Who have nowhere
To eat,
No place to sleep,
The tearless
Who cannot
Weep.

One

Lonely
As the wind
On the Lincoln
Prairies.

Lonely
As a bottle of licker
On a table
All by itself.

Desert

Anybody
Better than
Nobody.

In the barren dusk
Even the snake
That spirals
'Terror on the sand—

Better than nobody
In this lonely
Land.

A House in Taos

Rain

Thunder of the Rain God:
    And we three
    Smitten by beauty.

Thunder of the Rain God:
    And we three
    Weary, weary.

Thunder of the Rain God:
    And you, she, and I
    Waiting for nothingness.

Do you understand the stillness
    Of this house
    In Taos
Under the thunder of the Rain God?

Sun

That there should be a barren garden
About this house in Taos
Is not so strange,
But that there should be three barren hearts
In this one house in Taos—
Who carries ugly things to show the sun?

Moon

Did you ask for the beaten brass of the moon?
We can buy lovely things with money,
You, she, and I,
Yet you seek,
As though you could keep,
This unbought loveliness of moon.

Wind

Touch our bodies, wind.
Our bodies are separate, individual things.
Touch our bodies, wind,
But blow quickly
Through the red, white, yellow skins
Of our bodies
To the terrible snarl,
Not mine,
Not yours,
Not hers,
But all one snarl of souls.
Blow quickly, wind,
Before we run back
Into the windlessness—
With our bodies—
Into the windlessness
Of our house in Taos.

Demand

Listen!
Dear dream of utter aliveness—
Touching my body of utter death—
Tell me, O quickly! dream of aliveness,
The flaming source of your bright breath.
Tell me, O dream of utter aliveness—
Knowing so well the wind and the sun—
  Where is this light
  Your eyes see forever?
  And what is this wind
  You touch when you run?

Dream

Last night I dreamt
This most strange dream,
And everywhere I saw
What did not seem could ever be:

You were not there with me!

Awake,
I turned
And touched you
Asleep,
Face to the wall.

I said,
How dreams
Can lie!

But you were not there at all!

Night: Four Songs

Night of the two moons
And the seventeen stars,
Night of the day before yesterday
And the day after tomorrow,
Night of the four songs unsung:
    Sorrow! Sorrow!
    Sorrow! Sorrow!

Luck

Sometimes a crumb falls
From the tables of joy,
Sometimes a bone
Is flung.

To some people
Love is given,
To others
Only heaven.

Old Walt

Old Walt Whitman
Went finding and seeking,
Finding less than sought
Seeking more than found,
Every detail minding
Of the seeking or the finding.

Pleasured equally
In seeking as in finding,
Each detail minding,
Old Walt went seeking
And finding.

Kid in the Park

Lonely little question mark
on a bench in the park:

See the people passing by?
See the airplanes in the sky?
See the birds
flying home
before
dark?

Home's just around
the corner
there—
but not really
anywhere.

Song for Billie Holiday

What can purge my heart
>> Of the song
>> And the sadness?
What can purge my heart
>> But the song
>> Of the sadness?
What can purge my heart
>> Of the sadness
>> Of the song?

Do not speak of sorrow
With dust in her hair,
Or bits of dust in eyes
A chance wind blows there.
The sorrow that I speak of
Is dusted with despair.

Voice of muted trumpet,
Cold brass in warm air.
Bitter television blurred
By sound that shimmers—
>> Where?

Fantasy in Purple

Beat the drums of tragedy for me.
Beat the drums of tragedy and death.
And let the choir sing a stormy song
To drown the rattle of my dying breath.

Beat the drums of tragedy for me,
And let the white violins whir thin and slow,
But blow one blaring trumpet note of sun
To go with me
                    to the darkness
                                where I go.

After Hours

Midnight Raffle

I put my nickel
In the raffle of the night.
Somehow that raffle
Didn't turn out right.

I lost my nickel.
I lost my time.
I got back home
Without a dime.

When I dropped that nickel
In the subway slot,
I wouldn't have dropped it,
Knowing what I got.

I could just as well've
Stayed home inside:
My bread wasn't buttered
On neither side.

What?

Some pimps wear summer hats
Into late fall
Since the money that comes in
Won't cover it all—
Suit, overcoat, shoes—
And hat, too!

Got to neglect something,
So what would you do?

Gone Boy

Playboy of the dawn,
Solid gone!
Out all night
Until 12—1—2 a.m.

Next day
When he should be gone
To work—
Dog-gone!
He ain't gone.

I'm all alone in this world, she said,
Ain't got nobody to share my bed,
Ain't got nobody to hold my hand—
The truth of the matter's
I ain't got no man.

Big Boy opened his mouth and said,
Trouble with you is
You ain't got no head!
If you had a head and used your mind
You could have *me* with you
All the time.

She answered, Babe, what must I do?

He said, Share your bed—
And your money, too.

Maybe

I asked you, baby,
If you understood—
You told me that you didn't,
But you thought you would.

Lover's Return

My old time daddy
Came back home last night.
His face was pale and
His eyes didn't look just right.

He says, "Mary, I'm
Comin' home to you—
So sick and lonesome
I don't know what to do."

Oh, men treats women
Just like a pair o' shoes—
You kicks 'em round and
Does 'em like you choose.

I looked at my daddy—
Lawd! and I wanted to cry.
He looked so thin—
Lawd! that I wanted to cry.
But the devil told me:
    Damn a lover
    Come home to die!

Miss Blues'es Child

If the blues would let me,
Lord knows I would smile.
If the blues would let me,
I would smile, smile, smile.
Instead of that I'm cryin'—
I must be Miss Blues'es child.

You were my moon up in the sky,
At night my wishing star.
I love you, oh, I love you so—
But you have gone so far!

Now my days are lonely,
And night-time drives me wild.
In my heart I'm crying,
I'm just Miss Blues'es child!

Trumpet Player

The Negro
With the trumpet at his lips
Has dark moons of weariness
Beneath his eyes
Where the smoldering memory
Of slave ships
Blazed to the crack of whips
About his thighs.

The Negro
With the trumpet at his lips
Has a head of vibrant hair
Tamed down,
Patent-leathered now
Until it gleams
Like jet—
Were jet a crown.

The music
From the trumpet at his lips
Is honey
Mixed with liquid fire.
The rhythm
From the trumpet at his lips
Is ecstasy
Distilled from old desire—

Desire
That is longing for the moon
Where the moonlight's but a spotlight
In his eyes,
Desire
That is longing for the sea

Where the sea's a bar-glass
Sucker size.

The Negro
With the trumpet at his lips
Whose jacket
Has a *fine* one-button roll,
Does not know
Upon what riff the music slips
Its hypodermic needle
To his soul—

But softly
As the tune comes from his throat
Trouble
Mellows to a golden note.

Monroe's Blues

Monroe's fell on evil days—
His woman and his friend is dead.
Monroe's fell on evil days,
Can't hardly get his bread.

Monroe sings a little blues,
His little blues is sad.
Monroe sings a little blues—
My woman and my friend is dead.

Stony Lonesome

They done took Cordelia
Out to stony lonesome ground.
Done took Cordelia
To stony lonesome,
Laid her down.
They done put Cordelia
Underneath that
Grassless mound.
    Ay-Lord!
      Ay-Lord!
        Ay-Lord!
She done left po' Buddy
To struggle by his self.
Po' Buddy Jones,
Yes, he's done been left.
She's out in stony lonesome,
Lordy! Sleepin' by herself.
    Cordelia's
      In stony
        Lonesome
          Ground!

Black Maria

Must be the Black Maria
That I see,
The Black Maria that I see—
But I hope it
Ain't comin' for me.

Hear that music playin' upstairs?
Aw, my heart is
Full of cares—
But that music playin' upstairs
Is for me.

Babe, did you ever
See the sun
Rise at dawnin' full of fun?
Says, did you ever see the sun rise
Full of fun, full of fun?
Then you know a new day's
Done begun.

Black Maria passin' by
Leaves the sunrise in the sky—
And a new day,
Yes, a new day's
Done begun!

Life Is Fine

Life Is Fine

I went down to the river,
I set down on the bank.
I tried to think but couldn't,
So I jumped in and sank.

I came up once and hollered!
I came up twice and cried!
If that water hadn't a-been so cold
I might've sunk and died.

> *But it was*
> *Cold in that water!*
> *It was cold!*

I took the elevator
Sixteen floors above the ground.
I thought about my baby
And thought I would jump down.

I stood there and I hollered!
I stood there and I cried!
If it hadn't a-been so high
I might've jumped and died.

> *But it was*
> *High up there!*
> *It was high!*

So since I'm still here livin',
I guess I will live on.
I could've died for love—
But for livin' I was born.

Though you may hear me holler,
And you may see me cry—
I'll be dogged, sweet baby,
If you gonna see me die.

Life is fine!
Fine as wine!
Life is fine!

Still Here

I've been scarred and battered.
My hopes the wind done scattered.
Snow has friz me, sun has baked me.
    Looks like between 'em
    They done tried to make me
Stop laughin', stop lovin', stop livin'—
    But I don't care!
    I'm still here!

Ballad of the Gypsy

I went to the Gypsy's.
Gypsy settin' all alone.
I said, Tell me, Gypsy,
When will my gal be home?

Gypsy said, Silver,
Put some silver in my hand
And I'll look into the future
And tell you all I can.

I crossed her palm with silver,
Then she started in to lie.
She said, Now, listen, Mister,
She'll be here by and by.

Aw, what a lie!

I been waitin' and a-waitin'
And she ain't come home yet.
Something musta happened
To make my gal forget.

Uh! I hates a lyin' Gypsy
Will take good money from you,
Tell you pretty stories
And take your money from you—

But if I was a Gypsy
I would take your money, too.

Me and the Mule

My old mule,
He's got a grin on his face.
He's been a mule so long
He's forgot about his race.

I'm like that old mule—
Black—and don't give a damn!
You got to take me
Like I am.

Kid Sleepy

Listen, Kid Sleepy,
Don't you want to run around
To the other side of the house
Where the shade is?
It's sunny here
And your skin'll turn
A reddish-purple in the sun.

Kid Sleepy said,
I don't care.

Listen, Kid Sleepy,
Don't you want to get up
And go to work down-
Town somewhere
To earn enough
For lunches and car fare?

Kid Sleepy said,
I don't care.

Or would you rather,
Kid Sleepy, just
Stay here?

Rather just
Stay here.

Little Lyric (*Of Great Importance*)

I wish the rent
Was heaven sent.

Fired

Awake all night with loving
The bright day caught me
Unawares—asleep.

"Late to work again,"
The boss man said.
"You're fired!"

So I went on back to bed—
And dreamed the sweetest dream
With Caledonia's arm
Beneath my head.

Midnight Dancer

Wine-maiden
Of the jazz-tuned night,
Lips
Sweet as purple dew,
Breasts
Like the pillows of all sweet dreams,
Who crushed
The grapes of joy
And dripped their juice
On you?

Blue Monday

No use in my going
Downtown to work today,
    It's eight,
    I'm late—
And it's marked down that-a-way.

Saturday and Sunday's
Fun to sport around.
But no use denying—
Monday'll get you down.

That old blue Monday
Will surely get you down.

Ennui

It's such a
Bore
Being always
Poor.

Mama and Daughter

Mama, please brush off my coat.
I'm going down the street.

Where're you going, daughter?

To see my sugar-sweet.

Who is your sugar, honey?
Turn around—I'll brush behind.

He is that young man, mama,
I can't get off my mind.

Daughter, once upon a time—
Let me brush the hem—
Your father, yes, he was the one!
I felt like that about him.

But it was a long time ago
He up and went his way.
I hope that wild young son-of-a-gun
Rots in hell today!

Mama, dad couldn't be still young.

He *was* young yesterday.
He *was* young when he—
Turn around!
So I can brush your back, I say!

Delinquent

Little Julie
Has grown quite tall.
Folks say she don't like
To stay home at all.

Little Julie
Has grown quite stout.
Folks say it's not just
Stomach sticking out.

Little Julie
Has grown quite wise—
A tiger, a lion, and an owl
In her eyes.

Little Julie
Says she don't care!
What she means is:
*Nobody cares
Anywhere.*

S-sss-ss-sh!

Her great adventure ended
As great adventures should
In life being created
Anew—and good.

> *Except the neighbors*
> *And her mother*
> *Did not think it good!*

Nature has a way
Of not caring much
About marriage
Licenses and such.

> *But the neighbors*
> *And her mother*
> *Cared very much!*

The baby came one morning,
Almost with the sun.

> *The neighbors—*
> *And its grandma—*
> *Were outdone!*

But mother and child
Thought it fun.

Homecoming

I went back in the alley
And I opened up my door.
All her clothes was gone:
She wasn't home no more.

I pulled back the covers,
I made down the bed.
A *whole* lot of room
Was the only thing I had.

Final Curve

When you turn the corner
And you run into *yourself*
Then you know that you have turned
All the corners that are left.

Little Green Tree

It looks like to me
My good-time days done past.
Nothin' in this world
Is due to last.

I used to play
And I played so dog-gone hard.
Now old age has
Dealt my bad-luck card.

I look down the road
And I see a little tree.
A little piece down the road.
I see a little tree.

Them cool green leaves
Is waitin' to shelter me.

O, *little tree!*

Crossing

It was that lonely day, folks,
When I walked all by myself.
My friends was all around me
But it was as if they'd left.
I went up on a mountain
In a high cold wind
And the coat that I was wearing
Was mosquito-netting thin.
I went down in the valley
And I crossed an icy stream
And the water I was crossing
Was no water in a dream
And the shoes I was wearing
No protection for that stream.
Then I stood out on a prairie
And as far as I could see
Wasn't nobody on that prairie
Looked like me.
It was that lonely day, folks,
I walked all by myself:
My friends was right there with me
But was just as if they'd left.

Widow Woman

Oh, that last long ride is a
Ride everybody must take.
Yes, that last long ride's a
Ride everybody must take.
And that final stop is a
Stop everybody must make.

When they put you in the ground and
They throw dirt in your face,
I say put you in the ground and
Throw dirt in your face,
That's one time, pretty papa,
You'll sure stay in your place.

You was a mighty lover and you
Ruled me many years.
A mighty lover, baby, cause you
Ruled me many years—
If I live to be a thousand
I'll never dry these tears.

I don't want nobody else and
Don't nobody else want me.
I say don't want nobody else
And don't nobody else want me—

Yet you never can tell when a
Woman like me is free!

Lament *over* Love

Misery

Play the blues for me.
Play the blues for me.
No other music
'Ll ease my misery.

Sing a soothin' song.
Said a soothin' song,
Cause the man I love's done
Done me wrong.

Can't you understand,
O, understand
A good woman's cryin'
For a no-good man?

Black gal like me,
Black gal like me
'S got to hear a blues
For her misery.

Ballad of the Fortune Teller

Madam could look in your hand—
Never seen you before—
And tell you more than
You'd want to know.

She could tell you about love,
And money, and such.
And she wouldn't
Charge you much.

A fellow came one day.
Madam took him in.
She treated him like
He was her kin.

Gave him money to gamble.
She gave him bread,
And let him sleep in her
Walnut bed.

Friends tried to tell her
Dave meant her no good.
Looks like she could've knowed it
If she only would.

He mistreated her terrible,
Beat her up bad.
Then went off and left her.
Stole all she had.

She tried to find out
What road he took.
There wasn't a trace
No way she looked.

That woman who could foresee
What *your* future meant,
Couldn't tell, to save her,
Where Dave went.

Cora

I broke my heart this mornin',
Ain't got no heart no more.
Next time a man comes near me
Gonna shut an' lock my door
Cause they treat me mean—
The ones I love.
They always treat me mean.

Down and Out

Baby, if you love me
Help me when I'm down and out.
If you love me, baby,
Help me when I'm down and out,
I'm a po' gal
Nobody gives a damn about.

The credit man's done took ma clothes
And rent time's nearly here.
I'd like to buy a straightenin' comb,
An' I need a dime fo' beer.

I need a dime fo' beer.

Young Gal's Blues

I'm gonna walk to the graveyard
'Hind ma friend Miss Cora Lee.
Gonna walk to the graveyard
'Hind ma dear friend Cora Lee
Cause when I'm dead some
Body'll have to walk behind me.

I'm goin' to the po' house
To see ma old Aunt Clew.
Goin' to the po' house
To see ma old Aunt Clew.
When I'm old an' ugly
I'll want to see somebody, too.

The po' house is lonely
An' the grave is cold.
O, the po' house is lonely,
The graveyard grave is cold.
But I'd rather be dead than
To be ugly an' old.

When love is gone what
Can a young gal do?
When love is gone, O,
What can a young gal do?
Keep on a-lovin' me, daddy,
Cause I don't want to be blue.

Ballad of the Girl Whose Name Is Mud

A girl with all that raising,
It's hard to understand
How she could get in trouble
With a no-good man.

The guy she gave her all to
Dropped her with a thud.
Now amongst decent people,
Dorothy's name is mud.

But nobody's seen her shed a tear,
Nor seen her hang her head.
Ain't even heard her murmur,
Lord, I wish I was dead!

No! The hussy's telling everybody—
Just as though it was no sin—
That if she had a chance
She'd do it agin'!

Hard Daddy

I went to ma daddy,
Says Daddy I have got the blues.
Went to ma daddy,
Says Daddy I have got the blues.
Ma daddy says, Honey,
Can't you bring no better news?

I cried on his shoulder but
He turned his back on me.
Cried on his shoulder but
He turned his back on me.
He said a woman's cryin's
Never gonna bother me.

I wish I had wings to
Fly like the eagle flies.
Wish I had wings to
Fly like the eagle flies.
I'd fly on ma man an'
I'd scratch out both his eyes.

Midwinter Blues

In the middle of the winter,
Snow all over the ground.
In the middle of the winter,
Snow all over the ground—
'Twas the night befo' Christmas
My good man turned me down.

Don't know's I'd mind his goin'
But he left me when the coal was low.
Don't know's I'd mind his goin'
But he left when the coal was low.
Now, if a man loves a woman
That ain't no time to go.

He told me that he loved me
But he must a been tellin' a lie.
He told me that he loved me.
He must a been tellin' a lie.
But he's the only man I'll
Love till the day I die.

I'm gonna buy me a rose bud
An' plant it at my back door,
Buy me a rose bud,
Plant it at my back door,
So when I'm dead they won't need
No flowers from the store.

Little Old Letter

It was yesterday morning
I looked in my box for mail.
The letter that I found there
Made me turn right pale.

Just a little old letter,
Wasn't even one page long—
But it made me wish
I was in my grave and gone.

I turned it over,
Not a word writ on the back.
I never felt so lonesome
Since I was born black.

Just a pencil and paper,
You don't need no gun nor knife—
A little old letter
Can take a person's life.

Lament over Love

I hope my child'll
Never love a man.
I say I hope my child'll
Never love a man.
Love can hurt you
Mo'n anything else can.

I'm goin' down to the river
An' I ain't goin' there to swim;
Down to the river,
Ain't goin' there to swim.
My true love's left me
And I'm goin' there to think about him.

Love is like whiskey,
Love is like red, red wine.
Love is like whiskey,
Like sweet red wine.
If you want to be happy
You got to love all the time.

I'm goin' up in a tower
Tall as a tree is tall,
Up in a tower
Tall as a tree is tall.
Gonna think about my man—
And let my fool-self fall.

Magnolia Flowers

Daybreak in Alabama

When I get to be a composer
I'm gonna write me some music about
Daybreak in Alabama
And I'm gonna put the purtiest songs in it
Rising out of the ground like a swamp mist
And falling out of heaven like soft dew.
I'm gonna put some tall tall trees in it
And the scent of pine needles
And the smell of red clay after rain
And long red necks
And poppy colored faces
And big brown arms
And the field daisy eyes
Of black and white black white black people
And I'm gonna put white hands
And black hands and brown and yellow hands
And red clay earth hands in it
Touching everybody with kind fingers
And touching each other natural as dew
In that dawn of music when I
Get to be a composer
And write about daybreak
In Alabama.

Cross

My old man's a white old man
And my old mother's black.
If ever I cursed my white old man
I take my curses back.

If ever I cursed my black old mother
And wished she were in hell,
I'm sorry for that evil wish
And now I wish her well.

My old man died in a fine big house.
My ma died in a shack.
I wonder where I'm gonna die,
Being neither white nor black?

Magnolia Flowers

The quiet fading out of life
In a corner full of ugliness.

I went lookin' for magnolia flowers
But I didn't find 'em.
I went lookin' for magnolia flowers in the dusk
And there was only this corner
Full of ugliness.

> *'Scuse me,*
> *I didn't mean to stump ma toe on you, lady.*

There ought to be magnolias
Somewhere in this dusk.

> *'Scuse me,*
> *I didn't mean to stump ma toe on you.*

Mulatto

>*I am your son, white man!*

Georgia dusk
And the turpentine woods.
One of the pillars of the temple fell.

>*You are my son!*
>*Like hell!*

The moon over the turpentine woods.
The Southern night
Full of stars,
Great big yellow stars.
  What's a body but a toy?
    Juicy bodies
    Of nigger wenches
    Blue black
    Against black fences.
    O, you little bastard boy,
    What's a body but a toy?
The scent of pine wood stings the soft night air.
>*What's the body of your mother?*
Silver moonlight everywhere.
>*What's the body of your mother?*
Sharp pine scent in the evening air.
      A nigger night,
      A nigger joy,
      A little yellow
      Bastard boy.

>*Naw, you ain't my brother.*
>*Niggers ain't my brother.*

Not ever.
Niggers ain't my brother.

The Southern night is full of stars,
Great big yellow stars.
O, sweet as earth,
Dusk dark bodies
Give sweet birth
To little yellow bastard boys.

Git on back there in the night,
You ain't white.

The bright stars scatter everywhere.
Pine wood scent in the evening air.
A nigger night,
A nigger joy.

I am your son, white man!

A little yellow
Bastard boy.

Southern Mammy Sings

Miss Gardner's in her garden.
Miss Yardman's in her yard.
Miss Michaelmas is at de mass
And I am gettin' tired!
    Lawd!
I am gettin' tired!

The nations they is fightin'
And the nations they done fit.
Sometimes I think that white folks
Ain't worth a little bit.
    No, m'am!
Ain't worth a little bit.

Last week they lynched a colored boy.
They hung him to a tree.
That colored boy ain't said a thing
But we all should be free.
    Yes, m'am!
We all should be free.

Not meanin' to be sassy
And not meanin' to be smart—
But sometimes I think that white folks
Just ain't got no heart.
    No, m'am!
Just ain't got no heart.

Ku Klux

They took me out
To some lonesome place.
They said, "Do you believe
In the great white race?"

I said, "Mister,
To tell you the truth,
I'd believe in anything
If you'd just turn me loose."

The white man said, "Boy,
Can it be
You're a-standin' there
A-sassin' me?"

They hit me in the head
And knocked me down.
And then they kicked me
On the ground.

A klansman said, "Nigger,
Look me in the face—
And tell me you believe in
The great white race."

West Texas

Down in West Texas where the sun
Shines like the evil one
I had a woman
And her name
Was Joe.

Pickin' cotton in the field
Joe said I wonder how it would feel
For us to pack up
Our things
And go?

So we cranked up our old Ford
And we started down the road
Where we was goin'
We didn't know—
Nor which way.

But West Texas where the sun
Shines like the evil one
Ain't no place
For a colored
Man to stay!

Share-Croppers

Just a herd of Negroes
Driven to the field,
Plowing, planting, hoeing,
To make the cotton yield.

When the cotton's picked
And the work is done
Boss man takes the money
And we get none,

Leaves us hungry, ragged
As we were before.
Year by year goes by
And we are nothing more

Than a herd of Negroes
Driven to the field—
Plowing life away
To make the cotton yield.

Ruby Brown

She was young and beautiful
And golden like the sunshine
That warmed her body.
And because she was colored
Mayville had no place to offer her,
Nor fuel for the clean flame of joy
That tried to burn within her soul.

One day,
Sitting on old Mrs. Latham's back porch
Polishing the silver,
She asked herself two questions
And they ran something like this:
What can a colored girl do
On the money from a white woman's kitchen?
And ain't there any joy in this town?

Now the streets down by the river
Know more about this pretty Ruby Brown,
And the sinister shuttered houses of the bottoms
Hold a yellow girl
Seeking an answer to her questions.
The good church folk do not mention
Her name any more.

But the white men,
Habitués of the high shuttered houses,
Pay more money to her now
Than they ever did before,
When she worked in their kitchens.

Roland Hayes Beaten (*Georgia: 1942*)

Negroes,
Sweet and docile,
Meek, humble, and kind:
Beware the day
They change their minds!

Wind
In the cotton fields,
Gentle breeze:
Beware the hour
It uproots trees!

Uncle Tom

Within—
The beaten pride.
Without—
The grinning face,
The low, obsequious,
Double bow,
The sly and servile grace
Of one the white folks
Long ago
Taught well
To know his
Place.

Porter

I must say
Yes, sir,
To you all the time.
Yes, sir!
Yes, sir!
All my days
Climbing up a great big mountain
Of yes, sirs!

Rich old white man
Owns the world.
Gimme yo' shoes
To shine.

Yes, sir!

Blue Bayou

I went walkin'
By the blue bayou
And I saw the sun go down.
I thought about old Greeley
And I thought about Lou
And I saw the sun go down.

    White man
    Makes me work all day
    And I work too hard
    For too little pay—
    Then a white man
    Takes my woman away.

I'll kill old Greeley.

    The blue bayou
    Turns red as fire.
    Put the black man
    On a rope
    And pull him higher!

I saw the sun go down.

    Put him on a rope
    And pull him higher!

    The blue bayou's
    A pool of fire.
And I saw the sun go down,
    Down,
        Down,
Lawd, I saw the sun go down!

Silhouette

Southern gentle lady,
Do not swoon.
They've just hung a black man
In the dark of the moon.

They've hung a black man
To a roadside tree
In the dark of the moon
For the world to see
How Dixie protects
Its white womanhood.

Southern gentle lady,
    Be good!
    Be good!

Song for a Dark Girl

Way Down South in Dixie
    (Break the heart of me)
They hung my black young lover
    To a cross roads tree.

Way Down South in Dixie
    (Bruised body high in air)
I asked the white Lord Jesus
    What was the use of prayer.

Way Down South in Dixie
    (Break the heart of me)
Love is a naked shadow
    On a gnarled and naked tree.

The South

The lazy, laughing South
With blood on its mouth.
The sunny-faced South,
    Beast-strong,
    Idiot-brained.
The child-minded South
Scratching in the dead fire's ashes
For a Negro's bones.
    Cotton and the moon,
    Warmth, earth, warmth,
    The sky, the sun, the stars,
    The magnolia-scented South.
Beautiful, like a woman,
Seductive as a dark-eyed whore,
    Passionate, cruel,
    Honey-lipped, syphilitic—
    That is the South.
And I, who am black, would love her
But she spits in my face.
And I, who am black,
Would give her many rare gifts
But she turns her back upon me.
    So now I seek the North—
    The cold-faced North,
    For she, they say,
    Is a kinder mistress,
And in her house my children
May escape the spell of the South.

Bound No'th Blues

Goin' down the road, Lawd,
Goin' down the road.
Down the road, Lawd,
Way, way down the road.
Got to find somebody
To help me carry this load.

Road's in front o' me,
Nothin' to do but walk.
Road's in front o' me,
Walk . . . an' walk . . . an' walk.
I'd like to meet a good friend
To come along an' talk.

Hates to be lonely,
Lawd, I hates to be sad.
Says I hates to be lonely,
Hates to be lonely an' sad,
But ever friend you finds seems
Like they try to do you bad.

Road, road, road, O!
Road, road . . . road . . . road, road!
Road, road, road, O!
On the no'thern road.
These Mississippi towns ain't
Fit fer a hoppin' toad.

Name *in* Uphill Letters

One-Way Ticket

I pick up my life
And take it with me
And I put it down in
Chicago, Detroit,
Buffalo, Scranton,
Any place that is
North and East—
And not Dixie.

I pick up my life
And take it on the train
To Los Angeles, Bakersfield,
Seattle, Oakland, Salt Lake,
Any place that is
North and West—
And not South.

I am fed up
With Jim Crow laws,
People who are cruel
And afraid,
Who lynch and run,
Who are scared of me
And me of them.

I pick up my life
And take it away
On a one-way ticket—
Gone up North,
Gone out West,
Gone!

Migrant

(*Chicago*)

Daddy-o
Buddy-o
Works at the foundry.
Daddy-o
Buddy-o
Rides the State Street street car,
Transfers to the West Side,
Polish, Bohunk, Irish,
Grabs a load of sunrise
As he rides out on the prairie,
Never knew DuSable,
Has a lunch to carry.

Iron lifting iron
Makes iron of chocolate muscles.
Iron lifting iron
Makes hammer beat of drum beat
And the heat
Moulds and melts and moulds it
On red heart become an anvil
Until a glow is lighted
In the eyes once soft benighted
And the cotton field is frightened
A thousand miles away.

They draw up restrictive covenants
In Australia, too, they say.
Our President
Takes up important matters
Still left by V-J Day.
Congress cases Russia.

The *Tribune*'s hair
Turns gray.

Daddy-o
Buddy-o
Signs his name
In uphill letters
On the check that is his pay.
But if he wasn't in a hurry
He wouldn't write so
Bad that way,
Daddy-o.

Summer Evening (*Calumet Avenue*)

Mothers pass,
Sweet watermelon in a baby carriage,
Black seed for eyes
And a rose pink mouth.
Pimps in gray go by,
Boots polished like a Murray head,
Or in reverse
Madam Walker
On their shoe tips.
I. W. Harper
Stops to listen to gospel songs
From a tent at the corner
Where the carnival is Christian.
Jitneys go by
Full of chine bones in dark glasses,
And a blind man plays an accordion
Gurgling *Jericho.*

Theresa Belle Aletha
Throws a toothpick from her window,
And the four bells she's awaiting
Do not ring, not even murmur.
But maybe before midnight
The tamale man will come by,
And if Uncle Mac brings beer
Night will pull its slack taut
And wrap a string around its finger
So as not to forget
That tomorrow is Monday.

A *dime on those two bottles.*
Yes, they are yours,
Too!

And in another week
It will again
Be Sunday.

Graduation

Cinnamon and rayon,
Jet and coconut eyes,
Mary Lulu Jackson
Smooths the skirt
At her thighs.

Mama, portly oven,
Brings remainders from the kitchen
Where the people all are icebergs
Wrapped in checks and wealthy.

DIPLOMA in its new frame:
Mary Lulu Jackson,
Eating chicken,
Tells her mama she's a typist
And the clicking of the keys
Will spell the name
Of a job in a fine office
Far removed from basic oven,
Cookstoves,
And iceberg's kitchen.

Mama says, *Praise Jesus!*
Until then
I'll bring home chicken!

The DIPLOMA bursts its frame
To scatter star-dust in their eyes.

Mama says, *Praise Jesus!*
The colored race will rise!

Mama says,
Praise Jesus!

Then,
Because she's tired,
She sighs.

Interne at Provident

White coats
White aprons
White dresses
White shoes
Pain and a learning
To take away to Alabama.
Practice on a State Street cancer,
Practice on a stockyards rupture,
Practice on the small appendix
Of 26-girl at the corner,
Learning skills of surgeons
Brown and wonderful with longing
To cure ills of Africa,
Democracy,
And mankind,
Also ills quite common
Among all who stand on two feet.

Brown hands
Black hands
Golden hands in white coat,
Nurses' hands on suture.
Miracle maternity:
Pain on hind legs rising,
Pain tamed and subsiding
Like a mule broke to the halter.

Charity's checked money
Aids triumphant entry squalling
After bitter thrust of bearing
Chocolate and blood:

Projection of a day!

Tears of joy
And Coca-Cola
Twinkle on the rubber gloves
He's wearing.
A crown of sweat
Gleams on his forehead.

In the white moon
Of the amphitheatre
Magi are staring.

The light on the Palmolive Building
Shines like a star in the East.
Nurses turn glass doorknobs
Opening into corridors.

A mist of iodine and ether
Follows the young doctor,
Cellophanes his long stride,
Cellophanes his future.

Railroad Avenue

Dusk dark
On Railroad Avenue.
Lights in the fish joints,
Lights in the pool rooms.
A box-car some train
Has forgotten
In the middle of the
Block.
A player piano,
A victrola.
    942
    Was the number.

A boy
Lounging on a corner.
A passing girl
With purple powdered skin.
    Laughter
    Suddenly
    Like a taut drum.
    Laughter
    Suddenly
    Neither truth nor lie.
    Laughter
Hardening the dusk dark evening.
    Laughter
Shaking the lights in the fish joints,
Rolling white balls in the pool rooms,
And leaving untouched the box-car
Some train has forgotten.

Mother to Son

Well, son, I'll tell you:
Life for me ain't been no crystal stair.
It's had tacks in it,
And splinters,
And boards torn up,
And places with no carpet on the floor—
Bare.
But all the time
I'se been a-climbin' on,
And reachin' landin's,
And turnin' corners,
And sometimes goin' in the dark
Where there ain't been no light.
So boy, don't you turn back.
Don't you set down on the steps
'Cause you finds it's kinder hard.
Don't you fall now—
For I'se still goin', honey,
I'se still climbin',
And life for me ain't been no crystal stair.

Stars

O, sweep of stars over Harlem streets,
O, little breath of oblivion that is night.
    A city building
    To a mother's song.
    A city dreaming
    To a lullaby.
Reach up your hand, dark boy, and take a star.
Out of the little breath of oblivion
    That is night,
    Take just
    One star.

To Be Somebody

Little girl
Dreaming of a baby grand piano
(Not knowing there's a Steinway bigger, bigger)
Dreaming of a baby grand to play
That stretches paddle-tailed across the floor,
Not standing upright
Like a bad boy in the corner,
But sending music
Up the stairs and down the stairs
And out the door
To confound even Hazel Scott
Who might be passing!

Oh!

Little boy
Dreaming of the boxing gloves
Joe Louis wore,
The gloves that sent
Two dozen men to the floor.
Knockout!
Bam! Bop! Mop!

There's always room,
They say,
At the top.

Note on Commercial Theatre

You've taken my blues and gone—
You sing 'em on Broadway
And you sing 'em in Hollywood Bowl,
And you mixed 'em up with symphonies
And you fixed 'em
So they don't sound like me.
Yep, you done taken my blues and gone.

You also took my spirituals and gone.
You put me in *Macbeth* and *Carmen Jones*
And all kinds of *Swing Mikados*
And in everything but what's about me—
But someday somebody'll
Stand up and talk about me,
And write about me—
Black and beautiful—
And sing about me,
And put on plays about me!
I reckon it'll be
Me myself!

Yes, it'll be me.

Puzzled

Here on the edge of hell
Stands Harlem—
Remembering the old lies,
The old kicks in the back,
The old, *Be patient*,
They told us before.

Sure, we remember.
Now, when the man at the corner store
Says sugar's gone up another two cents,
And bread one,
And there's a new tax on cigarettes—
We remember the job we never had,
Never could get,
And can't have now
Because we're colored.

So we stand here
On the edge of hell
In Harlem
And look out on the world
And wonder
What we're gonna do
In the face of
What we remember.

Seashore through Dark Glasses (*Atlantic City*)

Beige sailors with large noses
Binocular the Atlantic.

At Club Harlem it's eleven
And seven cats go frantic.
Two parties from Philadelphia
Dignify the place
And murmur:

Such Negroes
disgrace the race!

On Artic Avenue
Sea food joints
Scent salty-colored
Compass points.

Baby

Albert!
Hey, Albert!
Don't you play in dat road.
　　You see dem trucks
　　A-goin' by.
　　One run ovah you
　　An' you die.
Albert, don't you play in dat road.

Merry-Go-Round

Colored child at carnival:

Where is the Jim Crow section
On this merry-go-round,
Mister, cause I want to ride?
Down South where I come from
White and colored
Can't sit side by side.
Down South on the train
There's a Jim Crow car.
On the bus we're put in the back—
But there ain't no back
To a merry-go-round!
Where's the horse
For a kid that's black?

Elevator Boy

I got a job now
Runnin' an elevator
In the Dennison Hotel in Jersey.
Job ain't no good though.
No money around.
    Jobs are just chances
    Like everything else.
    Maybe a little luck now,
    Maybe not.
    Maybe a good job sometimes:
    Step out o' the barrel, boy.
Two new suits an'
A woman to sleep with.
    Maybe no luck for a long time.
    Only the elevators
    Goin' up an' down,
    Up an' down,
    Or somebody else's shoes
    To shine,
    Or greasy pots in a dirty kitchen.
I been runnin' this
Elevator too long.
Guess I'll quit now.

Who But the Lord?

I looked and I saw
That man they call the Law.
He was coming
Down the street at me!
I had visions in my head
Of being laid out cold and dead,
Or else murdered
By the third degree.

I said, O, *Lord, if you can,*
Save me from that man!
Don't let him make a pulp out of me!
But the Lord he was not quick.
The Law raised up his stick
And beat the living hell
Out of me!

Now, I do not understand
Why God don't protect a man
From police brutality.
Being poor and black,
I've no weapon to strike back
So who but the Lord
Can protect me?

Third Degree

Hit me! Jab me!
Make me say I did it.
Blood on my sport shirt
And my tan suede shoes.

Faces like jack-o'-lanterns
In gray slouch hats.

Slug me! Beat me!
Scream jumps out
Like blow-torch.
Three kicks between the legs
That kill the kids
I'd make tomorrow.

Bars and floor skyrocket
And burst like Roman candles.

When you throw
Cold water on me,
I'll sign the
Paper. . . .

Ballad of the Man Who's Gone

No money to bury him.
The relief gave Forty-Four.
The undertaker told 'em,
You'll need Sixty more

For a first-class funeral,
A hearse and two cars—
And maybe your friends'll
Send some flowers.

His wife took a paper
And went around.
Everybody that gave something
She put 'em down.

She raked up a Hundred
For her man that was dead.
His buddies brought flowers.
A funeral was had.

A minister preached—
And charged Five
To bless him dead
And praise him alive.

Now that he's buried—
God rest his soul—
Reckon there's no charge
For graveyard mold.

I wonder what makes
A funeral so high?
A poor man ain't got
No business to die.

Madam *to* You

Madam's Past History

My name is Johnson—
Madam Alberta K.
The Madam stands for business.
I'm smart that way.

I had a
HAIR-DRESSING PARLOR
Before
The depression put
The prices lower.

Then I had a
BARBECUE STAND
'Till I got mixed up
With a no-good man.

Cause I had a insurance
The WPA
Said, We can't use you
Wealthy that way.

I said,
DON'T WORRY 'BOUT ME!
Just like the song,
You WPA folks take care of yourself—
And I'll get along.

I do cooking,
Day's work, too!
Alberta K. Johnson—
Madam to you.

Madam and Her Madam

I worked for a woman,
She wasn't mean—
But she had a twelve-room
House to clean.

Had to get breakfast,
Dinner, and supper, too—
Then take care of her children
When I got through.

Wash, iron, and scrub,
Walk the dog around—
It was too much,
Nearly broke me down.

I said, Madam,
Can it be
You trying to make a
Pack-horse out of me?

She opened her mouth.
She cried, Oh, no!
You know, Alberta,
I love you so!

I said, Madam,
That may be true—
But I'll be dogged
If I love you!

Madam's Calling Cards

I had some cards printed
The other day.
They cost me more
Than I wanted to pay.

I told the man
I wasn't no mint,
But I hankered to see
My name in print.

MADAM JOHNSON,
ALBERTA K.
He said, Your name looks good
Madam'd that way.

Shall I use Old English
Or a Roman letter?
I said, Use American.
American's better.

There's nothing foreign
To my pedigree:
Alberta K. Johnson—
American that's me.

Madam and the Rent Man

The rent man knocked.
He said, Howdy-do?
I said, What
Can I do for you?
He said, You know
Your rent is due.

I said, Listen,
Before I'd pay
I'd go to Hades
And rot away!

The sink is broke,
The water don't run,
And you ain't done a thing
You promised to've done.

Back window's cracked,
Kitchen floor squeaks,
There's rats in the cellar,
And the attic leaks.

He said, Madam,
It's not up to me.
I'm just the agent,
Don't you see?

I said, Naturally,
You pass the buck.
If it's money you want
You're out of luck.

He said, Madam,
I ain't pleased!
I said, Neither am I.

So we agrees!

Madam and the Number Writer

Number runner
Come to my door.
I had swore
I wouldn't play no more.

He said, Madam,
6–0–2
Looks like a likely
Hit for you.

I said, Last night,
I dreamed 7–0–3.
He said, That might
Be a hit for me.

He played a dime,
I played, too,
Then we boxed 'em.
Wouldn't you?

But the number that day
Was 3–2–6—
And we both was in
The *same* old fix.

I said, I swear I
Ain't gonna play no more
Till I get over
To the other shore—

Then I can play
On them golden streets

Where the number not only
Comes out—but repeats!

The runner said, Madam,
That's all very well—
But suppose
You goes to hell?

Madam and the Phone Bill

You say I O.K.ed
LONG DISTANCE?
O.K.ed it when?
My goodness, Central,
That was *then!*

I'm mad and disgusted
With that Negro now.
I don't pay no REVERSED
CHARGES nohow.

You say, I will pay it—
Else you'll take out my phone?
You better let
My phone alone.

I didn't ask him
To telephone me.
Roscoe knows darn well
LONG DISTANCE
Ain't free.

If I ever catch him,
Lawd, have pity!
Calling me up
From Kansas City

Just to say he loves me!
I knowed that was so.
Why didn't he tell me some'n
I don't know?

For instance, what can
Them other girls do
That Alberta K. Johnson
Can't do—*and more, too?*

What's that, Central?
You say you don't care
Nothing about my
Private affair?

Well, even less about your
PHONE BILL does I care!

Un-humm-m! . . . Yes!
You say I gave my O.K.?
Well, that O.K. you may keep—

But I *sure* ain't gonna pay!

Madam and the Charity Child

Once I adopted
A little girl child.
She grew up and got ruint,
Nearly drove me wild.

Then I adopted
A little boy.
He used a switch-blade
For a toy.

What makes these charity
Children so bad?
Ain't had no luck
With none I had.

Poor little things,
Born behind the 8-rock,
With parents that don't even
Stop to take stock.

The county won't pay me
But a few bucks a week.
Can't raise no child on that,
So to speak.

And the lady from the
Juvenile Court
Always coming around
Wanting a report.

Last time I told her,
Report, my eye!
Things is bad—
You figure out why!

Madam and the Fortune Teller

Fortune teller looked in my hand.
Fortune teller said,
Madam, It's just good luck
You ain't dead.

Fortune teller squeeze my hand.
She squinted up her eyes.
Fortune teller said,
Madam, you ain't wise.

I said, Please explain to me
What you mean by that?
She said, You must recognize
Where your fortune's at.

I said, Madam, tell me—
For she was *Madam*, too—
Where *is* my fortune at?
I'll pay some mind to you.

She said, Your fortune, honey,
Lies right in yourself.
You ain't gonna find it
On nobody else's shelf.

I said, What *man* you're talking 'bout?
She said, Madam! Be calm—
For one more dollar and a half,
I'll read your other palm.

Madam and the Wrong Visitor

A man knocked three times.
I never seen him before.
He said, Are you Madam?
I said, What's the score?

He said, I reckon
You don't know my name,
But I've come to call
On you just the same.

I stepped back
Like he had a charm.
He said, I really
Don't mean no harm.

I'm just Old Death
And I thought I might
Pay you a visit
Before night.

He said, You're Johnson—
Madam Alberta K.?
I said, Yes—but *Alberta*
Ain't goin' with you today!

No sooner had I told him
Than I awoke.
The doctor said, Madam,
Your fever's broke—

Nurse, put her on a diet,
And buy her some chicken.
I said, Better buy *two*—
Cause I'm still here kickin'!

Madam and the Minister

Reverend Butler came by
My house last week.
He said, Have you got
A little time to speak?

He said, I am interested
In your soul.
Has it been saved,
Or is your heart stone-cold?

I said, Reverend,
I'll have you know
I was baptized
Long ago.

He said, What have you
Done since then?
I said, None of your
Business, friend.

He said, Sister
Have you back-slid?
I said, It felt good—
If I did!

He said, Sister,
Come time to die,
The Lord will surely
Ask you why!
I'm gonna pray
For you!
Goodbye!

I felt kinder sorry
I talked that way
After Rev. Butler
Went away—
So I ain't in no mood
For sin today.

Madam and Her Might-Have-Been

I had two husbands.
I could of had three—
But my Might-Have-Been
Was too good for me.

When you grow up the hard way
Sometimes you don't know
What's too good to be true,
Just might be so.

He worked all the time,
Spent his money on me—
First time in my life
I had anything free.

I said, Do you love me?
Or am I mistaken?
You're always giving
And never taking.

He said, Madam, I swear
All I want is you.
Right then and there
I knowed we was through!

I told him, Jackson,
You better leave—
You got some'n else
Up your sleeve:

When you think you got bread
It's always a stone—

Nobody loves nobody
For yourself alone.

He said, In me
You've got no trust.
I said, I don't want
My heart to bust.

Madam and the Census Man

The census man,
The day he came round,
Wanted my name
To put it down.

I said, JOHNSON,
ALBERTA K.
But he hated to write
The K that way.

He said, What
Does K stand for?
I said, K—
And nothing more.

He said, I'm gonna put it
K—A—Y.
I said, If you do,
You lie.

My mother christened me
ALBERTA K.
You leave my name
Just that way!

He said, Mrs.,
(With a snort)
Just a K
Makes your name too short.

I said, I don't
Give a damn!

Leave me and my name
Just like I am!

Furthermore, rub out
That MRS., too—
I'll have you know
I'm *Madam* to you!

Montage
of a Dream
Deferred

Dream Boogie

Good morning, daddy!
Ain't you heard
The boogie-woogie rumble
Of a dream deferred?

Listen closely:
You'll hear their feet
Beating out and beating out a—

>   *You think*
>   *It's a happy beat?*

Listen to it closely:
Ain't you heard
something underneath
like a—

>   *What did I say?*

Sure,
I'm happy!
Take it away!

>   *Hey, pop!*
>   *Re-bop!*
>   *Mop!*

>   *Y-e-a-h!*

Parade

Seven ladies
and seventeen gentlemen
at the Elks Club Lounge
planning planning a parade:
Grand Marshal in his white suit
will lead it.
Cadillacs with dignitaries
will precede it.
And behind will come
with band and drum
on foot . . . on foot . . .
on foot . . .

Motorcycle cops,
white,
will speed it
out of sight
if they can:
Solid black,
can't be right.

Marching . . . marching . . .
marching . . .
noon till night . . .

> I never knew
> that many Negroes
> were on earth,
> did you?

> I never knew!

PARADE!

A chance to let

PARADE!

the whole world see

PARADE!

old black me!

Children's Rhymes

When I was a chile we used to play,
"One—two—buckle my shoe!"
and things like that. But now, Lord,
listen at them little varmints!

*By what sends
the white kids
I ain't sent:
I know I can't
be President.*

There is two thousand children
in this block, I do believe!

*What don't bug
them white kids
sure bugs me:
We knows everybody
ain't free!*

Some of these young ones is cert'ly bad—
One batted a hard ball right through my window
and my gold fish et the glass.

>*What's written down*
>*for white folks*
>*ain't for us a-tall:*
>*"Liberty And Justice—*
>*Huh—For All."*

>*Oop-pop-a-da!*
>*Skee! Daddle-de-do!*
>*Be-bop!*

Salt'peanuts!

>*De-dop!*

Sister

>That little Negro's married and got a kid.
>Why does he keep on foolin' around Marie?
>Marie's my sister—not married to me—
>But why does he keep on foolin' around Marie?
>Why don't she get a boy-friend
>I can understand—some decent man?

>>*Did it ever occur to you, son,*
>>*the reason Marie runs around with trash*
>>*is she wants some cash?*

>Don't decent folks have dough?

Unfortunately usually no!

Well, anyway, it don't have to be a married man.

Did it ever occur to you, boy,
that a woman does the best she can?

Comment on Stoop
So does a man.

Preference

I likes a woman
six or eight and ten years older'n myself.
I don't fool with these young girls.
Young girl'll say,
>   *Daddy, I want so-and-so.*
>   *I needs this, that, and the other.*
But a old woman'll say,
>   *Honey, what does YOU need?*
>   *I just drawed my money tonight*
>   *and it's all your'n.*
That's why I likes a older woman
who can appreciate me:
When she conversations you
it ain't forever, *Gimme!*

Necessity

Work?
I don't have to work.
I don't have to do nothing
but eat, drink, stay black, and die.
This little old furnished room's
so small I can't whip a cat
without getting fur in my mouth
and my landlady's so old
her features is all run together
and God knows she sure can overcharge—
Which is why I reckon I *does*
have to work after all.

Question

Said the lady, *Can you do*
what my other man can't do—
That is
love me, daddy—
and feed me, too?

Figurine

De-dop!

Buddy

That kid's my buddy,
still and yet
I don't see him much.
He works downtown for Twelve a week.
Has to give his mother Ten—
she says he can have
the other Two
to pay his carfare, buy a suit,
coat, shoes,
anything he wants out of it.

Juke Box Love Song

I could take the Harlem night
and wrap around you,
Take the neon lights and make a crown,
Take the Lenox Avenue busses,
Taxis, subways,
And for your love song tone their rumble down.
Take Harlem's heartbeat,
Make a drumbeat,
Put it on a record, let it whirl,
And while we listen to it play,
Dance with you till day—
Dance with you, my sweet brown Harlem girl.

Ultimatum

Baby, how come you can't see me
when I'm paying your bills
each and every week?

If you got somebody else,
tell me—
else I'll cut you off
without your rent.
I mean
without a cent.

Warning

Daddy,
don't let your dog
curb you!

Croon

I don't give a damn
For Alabam'
Even if it is my home.

New Yorkers

I was born here,
that's no lie, he said,
right here beneath God's sky.

I wasn't born here, she said,
I come—and why?
Where I come from
folks work hard
all their lives
until they die
and never own no parts
of earth nor sky
So I come up here.
Now what've I got?
    You!

She lifted up her lips
in the dark:
The same old spark!

Wonder

Early blue evening.
Lights ain't come on yet.
    Looky yonder!
    They come on now!

Easy Boogie

Down in the bass
That steady beat
Walking walking walking
Like marching feet.

Down in the bass
That easy roll,
Rolling like I like it
In my soul.

Riffs, smears, breaks.

Hey, Lawdy, Mama!
Do you hear what I said?
Easy like I rock it
In my bed!

Movies

The Roosevelt, Renaissance, Gem, Alhambra:
Harlem laughing in all the wrong places
    at the crocodile tears
    of crocodile art
    that you know
    in your heart
    is crocodile:

    (Hollywood
    laughs at me,
    black—
    so I laugh
    back.)

Tell Me

> Why should it be *my* loneliness,
> Why should it be *my* song,
> Why should it be *my* dream
> > deferred
> > overlong?

Not a Movie

> Well, they rocked him with road-apples
> because he tried to vote
> and whipped his head with clubs
> and he crawled on his knees to his house
> and he got the midnight train
> and he crossed that Dixie line
> now he's livin'
> on a 133rd.
>
> He didn't stop in Washington
> and he didn't stop in Baltimore
> neither in Newark on the way.
> Six knots was on his head
> but, thank God, he wasn't dead!
> And there ain't no Ku Klux
> on a 133rd.

Neon Signs

WONDER BAR

WISHING WELL

MONTEREY

MINTON'S
(ancient altar of Thelonious)

MANDALAY
Spots where the booted
and unbooted play

SMALL'S

CASBAH

SHALIMAR

.

. .

.

Mirror-go-round
where a broken glass
in the early bright
smears re-bop
sound

.

. .

.

Numbers

If I ever hit for a dollar
gonna salt every dime away
in the Post Office for a rainy day.

I ain't gonna
play back a cent.

(Of course, I might
combinate *a little*
with my rent.)

What? So Soon!

I believe my old lady's
pregnant again!

Fate must have
some kind of trickeration
to populate the
cullud nation!

Comment against Lamp Post
You call it fate?

Figurette
De-daddle-dy!
De-dop!

Motto

I play it cool
And dig all jive.
That's the reason
I stay alive.

My motto,
As I live and learn,
        is:
Dig And Be Dug
In Return.

Dead in There

Sometimes
A night funeral
Going by
Carries home
A cool bop daddy.

Hearse and flowers
Guarantee
He'll never hype
Another paddy.

It's hard to believe,
But dead in there,
He'll never lay a
Hype nowhere!

He's my ace-boy,
Gone away.
Wake up and live!
He used to say.

Squares
Who couldn't dig him,
Plant him now—
Out where it makes
No diff' no how.

Situation

When I rolled three 7's
in a row
I was scared to walk out
with the dough.

Dancer

Two or three things in the past
failed him
that had not failed people
of lesser genius.

In the first place
he didn't have much sense.
He was no good at making love
and no good at making money.
So he tapped,
    trucked,
    boogied,
    sanded,
    jittered,
until he made folks say,
    Looky yonder
    at that boy!
    Hey!
But being no good at lovin'—
the girls left him.
(When you're no good for dough they go.)
With no sense, just wonderful feet,
What could possibly be all-reet?
Did he get anywhere? No!

Even a great dancer
can't C.P.T.
a show.

Advice

Folks, I'm telling you,
birthing is hard
and dying is mean—
so get yourself
a little loving
in between.

Green Memory

A wonderful time—the War:
when money rolled in
and blood rolled out.
    But blood
    was far away
    from here—
Money was near.

Wine-O

Setting in the wine-house
Soaking up a wine-souse
Waiting for tomorrow to come—
Then
Setting in the wine-house
Soaking up a new souse.
Tomorrow . . .
Oh, hum!

Relief

My heart is aching
for them Poles and Greeks
on relief way across the sea
because I was on relief
once in 1933.

I know what relief can be—
it took me two years to get on WPA.
If the war hadn't come along
I wouldn't be out the barrel yet.
Now, I'm almost back in the barrel again.

To tell the truth,
if these white folks want to go ahead
and fight another war,
or even two,
the one to stop 'em won't be me.

Would you?

Ballad of the Landlord

Landlord, landlord,
My roof has sprung a leak.
Don't you 'member I told you about it
Way last week?

Landlord, landlord,
These steps is broken down.
When you come up yourself
It's a wonder you don't fall down.

Ten Bucks you say I owe you?
Ten Bucks you say is due?
Well, that's Ten Bucks more'n I'll pay you
Till you fix this house up new.

What? You gonna get eviction orders?
You gonna cut off my heat?
You gonna take my furniture and
Throw it in the street?

Um-huh! You talking high and mighty.
Talk on—till you get through.
You ain't gonna be able to say a word
If I land my fist on you.

Police! Police!
Come and get this man!
He's trying to ruin the government
And overturn the land!

Copper's whistle!
Patrol bell!
Arrest.

Precinct Station.
Iron cell.
Headlines in press:

MAN THREATENS LANDLORD

.
.   .

TENANT HELD NO BAIL

.
.   .

JUDGE GIVES NEGRO 90 DAYS IN COUNTY JAIL

Corner Meeting

Ladder, flag, and amplifier:
what the soap box
used to be.
The speaker catches fire
looking at their faces.
His words
jump down to stand
in listeners' places.

Projection

On the day when the Savoy
leaps clean over to Seventh Avenue
and starts jitterbugging
with the Renaissance,
on that day when Abyssinia Baptist Church
throws her enormous arms around
St. James Presbyterian
and 409 Edgecombe
stoops to kiss 12 West 133rd,
on that day—
Do, Jesus!
Manhattan Island will whirl
like a Dizzy Gillespie transcription
played by Inez and Timme.
On that day, Lord,
Sammy Davis and Marian Anderson
will sing a duet,
Paul Robeson
will team up with Jackie Mabley,
and Father Divine will say in truth,

Peace!
It's truly
wonderful!

Flatted Fifths

Little cullud boys with beards
re-bop be-bop mop and stop.

Little cullud boys with fears,
frantic, kick their draftee years
into flatted fifths and flatter beers
that at a sudden change become
sparkling Oriental wines
rich and strange
silken bathrobes with gold twines
and Heilbroner, Crawford,
Nat-undreamed-of Lewis combines
in silver thread and diamond notes
on trade-marks inside
Howard coats.

Little cullud boys in berets
    oop pop-a-da
horse a fantasy of days
    ool ya koo
and dig all plays.

Tomorrow

Tomorrow may be
a thousand years off:

TWO DIMES AND A NICKLE ONLY

says this particular
cigarette machine.

Others take a quarter straight.

Some dawns
wait.

Mellow

Into the laps
of black celebrities
white girls fall
like pale plums from a tree
beyond a high tension wall
wired for killing
which makes it
more thrilling.

Live and Let Live

Maybe it ain't right—
but the people of the night
will give even
a snake
a break.

Gauge

> Hemp . . .
> A stick . . .
> A roach . . .
> Straw . . .

Bar

> That whiskey will cook the egg.
> > *Say not so!*
> > *Maybe the egg*
> > *will cook the whiskey.*
> You ought to know!

Café: 3 A.M.

> Detectives from the vice squad
> with weary sadistic eyes
> spotting fairies.
> > *Degenerates,*
> > some folks say.
>
> > But God, Nature,
> > or somebody
> > made them that way.
>
> Police lady or Lesbian
> over there?
> > *Where?*

Drunkard

Voice grows thicker
as song grows stronger
as time grows longer until day
trying to forget to remember
the taste of day.

Street Song

Jack, if you got to be a rounder
Be a rounder right—
Just don't let mama catch you
Makin' rounds at night.

125th Street

Face like a chocolate bar
full of nuts and sweet.

Face like a jack-o'-lantern,
candle inside.

Face like slice of melon,
grin that wide.

Dive

Lenox Avenue
by daylight
runs to dive in the Park
but faster . . .
faster . . .
after dark.

Warning: Augmented

Don't let your dog curb you!
    Curb your doggie
    Like you ought to do,
But don't let that dog curb you!
    You may play folks cheap,
    Act rough and tough,
    But a dog can tell
    When you're full of stuff.
    Them little old mutts
    Look all scraggly and bad,
    But they got more sense
    Than some people ever had.
Cur dog, fice dog, kerry blue—
Just don't let your dog curb you!

Up-Beat

In the gutter
boys who try
might meet girls
on the fly

as out of the gutter
girls who will
may meet boys
copping a thrill
while from the gutter
both can rise:
But it requires
plenty eyes.

Jam Session

Letting midnight
out on bail
    pop-a-da
having been
detained in jail
    oop-pop-a-da
for sprinkling salt
on a dreamer's tail
    pop-a-da

Be-Bop Boys

Imploring Mecca
to achieve
six discs
with Decca.

Tag

> Little cullud boys
> with fears,
> frantic,
> nudge their draftee years.
>
> *Pop-a-da!*

Theme for English B

The instructor said,

> *Go home and write*
> *a page tonight.*
> *And let that page come out of you—*
> *Then, it will be true.*

I wonder if it's that simple?
I am twenty-two, colored, born in Winston-Salem.
I went to school there, then Durham, then here
to this college on the hill above Harlem.
I am the only colored student in my class.
The steps from the hill lead down into Harlem,
through a park, then I cross St. Nicholas,
Eighth Avenue, Seventh, and I come to the Y,
the Harlem Branch Y, where I take the elevator
up to my room, sit down, and write this page:

It's not easy to know what is true for you or me
at twenty-two, my age. But I guess I'm what
I feel and see and hear, Harlem, I hear you:
hear you, hear me—we two—you, me, talk on this page.
(I hear New York, too.) Me—who?

Well, I like to eat, sleep, drink, and be in love.
I like to work, read, learn, and understand life.
I like a pipe for a Christmas present,
or records—Bessie, bop, or Bach.
I guess being colored doesn't make me *not* like
the same things other folks like who are other races.
So will my page be colored that I write?
Being me, it will not be white.
But it will be
a part of you, instructor.
You are white—
yet a part of me, as I am a part of you.
That's American.
Sometimes perhaps you don't want to be a part of me.
Nor do I often want to be a part of you.
But we are, that's true!
As I learn from you,
I guess you learn from me—
although you're older—and white—
and somewhat more free.

This is my page for English B.

College Formal: Renaissance Casino

> Golden girl
> in a golden gown
> in a melody night
> in Harlem town
> lad tall and brown
> tall and wise

college boy smart
eyes in eyes
the music wraps
them both around
in mellow magic
of dancing sound
till they're the heart
of the whole big town
gold and brown

Low to High

How can you forget me?
But you do!
You said you was gonna take me
Up with you—
Now you've got your Cadillac,
you done forgot that you are black.
How can you forget me
When I'm you?

But you do.

How can you forget me,
fellow, say?
How can you low-rate me
this way?
You treat me like you damn well please,
Ignore me—though I pay your fees.
How can you forget me?

But you do.

Boogie: 1 a.m.

Good evening, daddy!
I know you've heard
The boogie-woogie rumble
Of a dream deferred
Trilling the treble
And twining the bass
Into midnight ruffles
Of cat-gut lace.

High to Low

God knows
We have our troubles, too—
One trouble is you:
you talk too loud,
cuss too loud,
look too black,
don't get anywhere,
and sometimes it seems
you don't even care.
The way you send your kids to school
stockings down,
(not Ethical Culture)
the way you shout out loud in church,
(not St. Phillips)
and the way you lounge on doorsteps
just as if you were down South,
(not at 409)
the way you clown—
the way, in other words,
you let me down—

me, trying to uphold the race
and you—
well, you can see,
we have our problems,
too, with you.

Lady's Boogie

See that lady
Dressed so fine?
She ain't got boogie-woogie
On her mind—

But if she was to listen
I bet she'd hear,
Way up in the treble
The tingle of a tear.

Be-Bach!

So Long

So long
is in the song
and it's in the way you're gone
but it's like a foreign language
in my mind
and maybe was I blind
I could not see

and would not know
you're gone so long
so long.

Deferred

This year, maybe, do you think I can graduate?
I'm already two years late.
Dropped out six months when I was seven,
a year when I was eleven,
then got put back when we come North.
To get through high at twenty's kind of late—
But maybe this year I can graduate.

Maybe now I can have that white enamel stove
I dreamed about when we first fell in love
eighteen years ago.
But you know,
rooming and everything
then kids,
cold-water flat and all that.
But now my daughter's married
And my boy's most grown—
quit school to work—
and where we're moving
there ain't no stove—
Maybe I can buy that white enamel stove!

Me, I always did want to study French.
It don't make sense—
I'll never go to France,

but night schools teach French.
Now at last I've got a job
where I get off at five,
in time to wash and dress,
so, si'l-vous plait, I'll study French!

Someday,
I'm gonna buy two new suits
at once!

All I want is
one more bottle of gin.

All I want is to see
my furniture paid for.

All I want is a wife who will
work with me and not against me. Say,
baby, could you see your way clear?

Heaven, heaven, is my home!
This world I'll leave behind
When I set my feet in glory
I'll have a throne for mine!

I want to pass the civil service.

I want a television set.

You know, as old as I am,
I ain't never
owned a decent radio yet?

I'd like to take up Bach.

> *Montage*
> *of a dream*
> *deferred.*

Buddy, have you heard?

Request

> Gimme $25.oo
> and the change.
> I'm going
> where the morning
> and the evening
> won't bother me.

Shame on You

If you're great enough
and clever enough
the government might honor you.
But the people will forget—
Except on holidays.

A movie house in Harlem named after Lincoln,
Nothing at all named after John Brown.

Black people don't remember
any better than white.

If you're not alive and kicking,
shame on you!

World War II

What a grand time was the war!
Oh, my, my!
What a grand time was the war!
My, my, my!
In wartime we had fun,
Sorry that old war is done!
What a grand time was the war,
My, my!

Echo:
Did
Somebody
Die?

Mystery

When a chile gets to be thirteen
and ain't seen Christ yet,
she needs to set on de moaner's bench
night and day.

Jesus, lover of my soul!

Hail, Mary, mother of God!

Let me to thy bosom fly!

Amen! Hallelujah!

Swing low, sweet chariot,
Coming for to carry me home.

Sunday morning where the rhythm flows,
how old nobody knows—
yet old as mystery,
older than creed,
basic and wondering
and lost as my need.

> *Eli, eli!*
>
> *Te deum!*
>
> *Mahomet!*
>
> *Christ!*

Father Bishop, Effendi, Mother Horne,
Father Divine, a Rabbi black
as black was born,
a jack-leg preacher, a Ph.D.

> *The mystery*
> *and the darkness*
> *and the song*
> *and me.*

Sliver of Sermon

When pimps out of loneliness cry:
　　Great God!
Whores in final weariness say:
　　Great God!
　　Oh, God!
　　My God!

　　Great
　　God!

Testimonial

If I just had a piano,
if I just had a organ,
if I just had a drum,
how I could praise my Lord!

But I don't need no piano,
　　neither organ
　　nor drum
for to praise my Lord!

Passing

On sunny summer Sunday afternoons in Harlem
when the air is one interminable ball game
and grandma cannot get her gospel hymns
from the Saints of God in Christ
on account of the Dodgers on the radio,

on sunny Sunday afternoons
when the kids look all new
and far too clean to stay that way,
and Harlem has its
washed-and-ironed-and-cleaned-best out,
the ones who've crossed the line
to live downtown
miss you,
Harlem of the bitter dream,
since their dream has
come true.

Nightmare Boogie

I had a dream
and I could see
a million faces
black as me!
A nightmare dream:
Quicker than light
All them faces
Turned dead white!
Boogie-woogie,
Rolling bass,
Whirling treble
of cat-gut lace.

Sunday by the Combination

I feel like dancin', baby,
till the sun goes down.

But I wonder where
the sunrise
Monday morning's gonna be?

I feel like dancin'!
Baby, dance with me!

Casualty

He was a soldier in the army,
But he doesn't walk like one.
He walks like his soldiering
Days are done.

Son! . . . Son!

Night Funeral in Harlem

Night funeral
In Harlem:

*Where did they get
Them two fine cars?*

Insurance man, he did not pay—
His insurance lapsed the other day—

Yet they got a satin box
For his head to lay.

  Night funeral
  In Harlem:

  Who was it sent
  That wreath of flowers?

Them flowers came
from that poor boy's friends—
They'll want flowers, too,
When they meet their ends.

  Night funeral
  In Harlem:

  Who preached that
  Black boy to his grave?

Old preacher-man
Preached that boy away—
Charged Five Dollars
His girl friend had to pay.

  Night funeral
  In Harlem:

When it was all over
And the lid shut on his head
and the organ had done played
and the last prayers been said
and six pallbearers

Carried him out for dead
And off down Lenox Avenue
That long black hearse done sped,
        The street light
        At his corner
        Shined just like a tear—
That boy that they was mournin'
Was so dear, so dear
To them folks that brought the flowers,
To that girl who paid the preacher man—
It was all their tears that made
        That poor boy's
        Funeral grand.

        Night funeral
        In Harlem.

Blues at Dawn

I don't dare start thinking in the morning.
I don't dare start thinking in the morning.
    If I thought thoughts in bed,
    Them thoughts would bust my head—
So I don't dare start thinking in the morning.

I don't dare remember in the morning
Don't dare remember in the morning.
    If I recall the day before,
    I wouldn't get up no more—
So I don't dare remember in the morning.

Dime

Chile, these steps is hard to climb.

Grandma, lend me a dime.

Montage of a dream deferred:

Grandma acts like
She ain't heard.

Chile, Granny ain't got no dime.

I might've knowed
It all the time.

Argument

White is right,
Yellow mellow,
Black, get back!

Do you believe that, Jack?

Sure do!

Then you're a dope
for which there ain't no hope.
Black is fine!
And, God knows,
It's mine!

Neighbor

Down home
he sets on a stoop
and watches the sun go by.
In Harlem
when his work is done
he sets in a bar with a beer.
He looks taller than he is
and younger than he ain't.
He looks darker than he is, too.
And he's smarter than he looks,

> *He ain't smart.*
> *That cat's a fool.*

Naw, he ain't neither.
He's a good man,
except that he talks too much.
In fact, he's a great cat.
But when he drinks,
he drinks fast.

> *Sometimes*
> *he don't drink.*

True,
he just
lets his glass
set there.

Evening Song

A woman standing in the doorway
Trying to make her where-with-all:
Come here, baby, darlin'!
Don't you hear me call?

If I was anybody's sister,
I'd tell her, *Gimme a place to sleep.*
But I ain't nobody's sister.
I'm just a poor lost sheep.

Mary, Mary, Mary,
Had a little lamb.
Well, I hope that lamb of Mary's
Don't turn out like I am.

Chord

Shadow faces
In the shadow night
Before the early dawn
Bops bright.

Fact

There's been an eagle on a nickel,
An eagle on a quarter, too.
But there ain't no eagle
On a dime.

Joe Louis

They worshipped Joe.
A school teacher
whose hair was gray
said:
> *Joe has sense enough to know*
> *He is a god.*
> *So many gods don't know.*

"They say". . ."They say". . ."They say". . .
But the gossips had no
"They say"
to latch onto
for Joe.

Subway Rush Hour

Mingled
breath and smell
so close
mingled
black and white
so near
no room for fear.

Brothers

We're related—you and I,
You from the West Indies,
I from Kentucky.

Kinsmen—you and I,
You from Africa,
I from the U.S.A.

Brothers—you and I.

Likewise

The Jews:
    Groceries
    Suits
    Fruits
    Watches
    Diamond rings
    THE DAILY NEWS
Jews sell me things.
Yom Kippur, no!
Shops all over Harlem
close up tight that night.

Some folks blame high prices on the Jews.
(Some folks blame too much on Jews.)
But in Harlem they don't answer back,
Just maybe shrug their shoulders,
"What's the use?"
What's the use
in Harlem?
What's the use?
What's the Harlem
use in Harlem
what's the lick?

266

Hey!
Baba-re-bop!
Mop!
On a be-bop kick!

Sometimes I think
Jews must have heard
the music of a
dream deferred.

Sliver

Cheap little rhymes
A cheap little tune
Are sometimes as dangerous
As a sliver of the moon.
A cheap little tune
To cheap little rhymes
Can cut a man's
Throat sometimes.

Hope

He rose up on his dying bed
and asked for fish.
His wife looked it up in her dream book
and played it.

Dream Boogie: Variation

Tinkling treble,
Rolling bass,
High noon teeth
In a midnight face,
Great long fingers
On great big hands,
Screaming pedals
Where his twelve-shoe lands,
Looks like his eyes
Are teasing pain,
A few minutes late
For the Freedom Train.

Harlem

What happens to a dream deferred?

Does it dry up
like a raisin in the sun?
Or fester like a sore—
And then run?
Does it stink like rotten meat?
Or crust and sugar over—
like a syrupy sweet?

Maybe it just sags
like a heavy load.

Or does it explode?

Good Morning

Good morning, daddy!
I was born here, he said,
watched Harlem grow
until colored folks spread
from river to river
across the middle of Manhattan
out of Penn Station
dark tenth of a nation,
planes from Puerto Rico,
and holds of boats, chico,
up from Cuba Haiti Jamaica,
in buses marked New York
from Georgia Florida Louisiana
to Harlem Brooklyn the Bronx
but most of all to Harlem
dusky sash across Manhattan
I've seen them come dark
    wondering
    wide-eyed
    dreaming
out of Penn Station—
but the trains are late.
The gates open—
Yet there're bars
at each gate.

    What happens
    to a dream deferred?

Daddy, ain't you heard?

Same in Blues

I said to my baby,
Baby, take it slow.
I can't, she said, I can't!
I got to go!

> There's a certain
> amount of traveling
> in a dream deferred.

Lulu said to Leonard,
I want a diamond ring.
Leonard said to Lulu,
You won't get a goddamn thing!

> A certain
> amount of nothing
> in a dream deferred.

Daddy, daddy, daddy,
All I want is you.
You can have me, baby—
but my lovin' days is through.

> A certain
> amount of impotence
> in a dream deferred.

Three parties
On my party line—
But that third party,
Lord, ain't mine!

There's liable
to be confusion
in a dream deferred.

From river to river,
Uptown and down,
There's liable to be confusion
when a dream gets kicked around.

Comment on Curb

You talk like
they don't kick
dreams around
downtown.

I expect they do—
But I'm talking about
Harlem to you!

Letter

Dear Mama,
*   Time I pay rent and get my food*
and laundry I don't have much left
but here is five dollars for you
to show you I still appreciates you.
My girl-friend send her love and say
she hopes to lay eyes on you sometime in life.

Mama, it has been raining cats and dogs up
here. Well, that is all so I will close.
               Your son baby
                   Respectably as ever,
                       Joe

Island

Between two rivers,
North of the park,
Like darker rivers
The streets are dark.

Black and white,
Gold and brown—
Chocolate-custard
Pie of a town.

Dream within a dream,
Our dream deferred.

Good morning, daddy!

Ain't you heard?

Words Like
Freedom

I, Too

I, too, sing America.

I am the darker brother.
They send me to eat in the kitchen
When company comes,
But I laugh,
And eat well,
And grow strong.

Tomorrow,
I'll be at the table
When company comes.
Nobody'll dare
Say to me,
"Eat in the kitchen,"
Then.

Besides,
They'll see how beautiful I am
And be ashamed—

I, too, am America.

Freedom Train

I read in the papers about the
    Freedom Train.
I heard on the radio about the
    Freedom Train.
I seen folks talkin' about the
    Freedom Train.
Lord, I been a-waitin' for the
    Freedom Train!

Down South in Dixie only train I see's
Got a Jim Crow car set aside for me.
I hope there ain't no Jim Crow on the Freedom Train,
No back door entrance to the Freedom Train,
No signs FOR COLORED on the Freedom Train,
No WHITE FOLKS ONLY on the Freedom Train.

    I'm gonna check up on this
        Freedom Train.

Who's the engineer on the Freedom Train?
Can a coal black man drive the Freedom Train?
Or am I still a porter on the Freedom Train?
Is there ballot boxes on the Freedom Train?
When it stops in Mississippi will it be made plain
Everybody's got a right to board the Freedom Train?

    Somebody tell me about this
        Freedom Train!

The Birmingham station's marked COLORED and WHITE.
The white folks go left, the colored go right—
They even got a segregated lane.
Is that the way to get aboard the Freedom Train?

I got to know about this
Freedom Train!

If my children ask me, *Daddy, please explain*
Why there's Jim Crow stations for the Freedom Train?
What shall I tell my children? . . . *You* tell me—
'Cause freedom ain't freedom when a man ain't free.

But maybe they explains it on the
Freedom Train.

When my grandmother in Atlanta, 83 and black,
Gets in line to see the Freedom,
Will some white man yell, *Get back!*
A Negro's got no business on the Freedom Track!

Mister, I thought it were the
Freedom Train!

Her grandson's name was Jimmy. He died at Anzio.
He died for real. It warn't no show.
The freedom that they carryin' on this Freedom Train,
Is it for real—or just a show again?

Jimmy wants to know about the
Freedom Train.

Will *his* Freedom Train come zoomin' down the track
Gleamin' in the sunlight for white and black?
Not stoppin' at no stations marked COLORED nor WHITE,
Just stoppin' in the fields in the broad daylight,
Stoppin' in the country in the wide-open air
Where there never was no Jim Crow signs nowhere,

No Welcomin' Committees, nor politicians of note,
No Mayors and such for which colored can't vote,
And nary a sign of a color line—
For the Freedom Train will be yours and mine!

Then maybe from their graves in Anzio
The G.I.'s who fought will say, *We wanted it so!*
Black men and white will say, *Ain't it fine?*
At home they got a train that's yours and mine!

> Then I'll shout, *Glory for the*
> *Freedom Train!*
> I'll holler, *Blow your whistle,*
> *Freedom Train!*
> *Thank God-A-Mighty! Here's the*
> *Freedom Train!*
> *Get on board our Freedom Train!*

Georgia Dusk

Sometimes there's a wind in the Georgia dusk
That cries and cries and cries
Its lonely pity through the Georgia dusk
Veiling what the darkness hides.

Sometimes there's blood in the Georgia dusk,
Left by a streak of sun,
A crimson trickle in the Georgia dusk.
Whose blood? . . . Everyone's.

Sometimes a wind in the Georgia dusk
Scatters hate like seed
To sprout its bitter barriers
Where the sunsets bleed.

Lunch in a Jim Crow Car

Get out the lunch-box of your dreams.
Bite into the sandwich of your heart,
And ride the Jim Crow car until it screams
Then—like an atom bomb—it bursts apart.

In Explanation of Our Times

The folks with no titles in front of their names
all over the world
are raring up and talking back
to the folks called Mister.

You say you thought everybody was called Mister?

No, son, not everybody.
In Dixie, often they won't call Negroes Mister.
In China before what happened
They had no intention of calling coolies Mister.
Dixie to Singapore, Cape Town to Hong Kong
the Misters won't call lots of other folks Mister.
They call them, Hey George!
                    Here, Sallie!
                    Listen, Coolie!
                    Hurry up, Boy!
                    And things like that.

George Sallie Coolie Boy gets tired sometimes.
So all over the world today
folks with not even Mister in front of their names
are raring up and talking back
to those called Mister.
From Harlem past Hong Kong talking back.

Shut up, says Gerald L. K. Smith.
Shut up, says the Governor of South Carolina.
Shut up, says the Governor of Singapore.
Shut up, says Strydom.

Hell no shut up! say the people
with no titles in front of their names.

Hell, no! It's time to talk back now!
History says it's time,
And the radio, too, foggy with propaganda
that says a mouthful
and don't mean half it says—
but is true anyhow:
    LIBERTY!
    FREEDOM!
    DEMOCRACY!
True anyhow no matter how many
Liars use those words.

The people with no titles in front of their names
hear those words and shout them back
at the Misters, Lords, Generals, Viceroys,
Governors of South Carolina, Gerald L. K. Strydoms.

    Shut up, people!
    Shut up! Shut up!
    Shut up, George!
    Shut up, Sallie!
    Shut up, Coolie!
    Shut up, Indian!
    Shut up, Boy!

George Sallie Coolie Indian Boy
black brown yellow bent down working
earning riches for the whole world
with no title in front of name
just man woman tired says:

    No shut up!
    Hell no shut up!

So, naturally, there's trouble
in these our times
because of people with no titles
in front of their names.

Africa

Sleepy giant,
You've been resting awhile.

Now I see the thunder
And the lightning
In your smile.
Now I see
The storm clouds
In your waking eyes:
The thunder,
The wonder,
And the young
Surprise.

Your every step reveals
The new stride
In your thighs.

Democracy

Democracy will not come
Today, this year
    Nor ever
Through compromise and fear.

I have as much right
As the other fellow has
    To stand
On my two feet
And own the land.

I tire so of hearing people say,
Let things take their course.
Tomorrow is another day.
I do not need my freedom when I'm dead.
I cannot live on tomorrow's bread.

    Freedom
    Is a strong seed
    Planted
    In a great need.
    I live here, too.
    I want freedom
    Just as you.

Consider Me

Consider me,
A colored boy,
Once sixteen,
Once five, once three,
Once nobody,
Now me.
Before me
Papa, mama,
Grandpa, grandma,
So on back
To original
Pa.

    (A capital letter there,
    He
    Being Mystery.)

Consider me,
Colored boy,
Downtown at eight,
Sometimes working late,
Overtime pay
To sport away,
Or save,
Or give my Sugar
For the things
She needs.

My Sugar,
Consider her
Who works, too—
Has to.
One don't make enough

For all the stuff
It takes to live.
Forgive me
What I lack,
Black,
Caught in a crack
That splits the world in two
From China
By way of Arkansas
To Lenox Avenue.

Consider me,
On Friday the eagle flies.
Saturday laughter, a bar, a bed.
Sunday prayers syncopate glory.
Monday comes,
To work at eight,
Late,
Maybe.

Consider me,
Descended also
From the
Mystery.

The Negro Mother

Children, I come back today
To tell you a story of the long dark way
That I had to climb, that I had to know
In order that the race might live and grow.
Look at my face—dark as the night—
Yet shining like the sun with love's true light.
I am the child they stole from the sand
Three hundred years ago in Africa's land.
I am the dark girl who crossed the wide sea
Carrying in my body the seed of the free.
I am the woman who worked in the field
Bringing the cotton and the corn to yield.
I am the one who labored as a slave,
Beaten and mistreated for the work that I gave—
Children sold away from me, husband sold, too.
No safety, no love, no respect was I due.
Three hundred years in the deepest South:
But God put a song and a prayer in my mouth.
God put a dream like steel in my soul.
Now, through my children, I'm reaching the goal.
Now, through my children, young and free,
I realize the blessings denied to me.
I couldn't read then. I couldn't write.
I had nothing, back there in the night.
Sometimes, the valley was filled with tears,
But I kept trudging on through the lonely years.
Sometimes, the road was hot with sun,
But I had to keep on till my work was done:
I *had* to keep on! No stopping for me—
I was the seed of the coming Free.
I nourished the dream that nothing could smother
Deep in my breast—the Negro mother.
I had only hope then, but now through you,

Dark ones of today, my dreams must come true:
All you dark children in the world out there,
Remember my sweat, my pain, my despair.
Remember my years, heavy with sorrow—
And make of those years a torch for tomorrow.
Make of my past a road to the light
Out of the darkness, the ignorance, the night.
Lift high my banner out of the dust.
Stand like free men supporting my trust.
Believe in the right, let none push you back.
Remember the whip and the slaver's track.
Remember how the strong in struggle and strife
Still bar you the way, and deny you life—
But march ever forward, breaking down bars.
Look ever upward at the sun and the stars.
Oh, my dark children, may my dreams and my prayers
Impel you forever up the great stairs—
For I will be with you till no white brother
Dares keep down the children of the Negro mother.

Refugee in America

There are words like *Freedom*
Sweet and wonderful to say.
On my heart-strings freedom sings
All day everyday.

There are words like *Liberty*
That almost make me cry.
If you had known what I knew
You would know why.

Freedom's Plow

When a man starts out with nothing,
When a man starts out with his hands
Empty, but clean,
When a man starts out to build a world,
He starts first with himself
And the faith that is in his heart—
The strength there,
The will there to build.

First in the heart is the dream.
Then the mind starts seeking a way.
His eyes look out on the world,
On the great wooded world,
On the rich soil of the world,
On the rivers of the world.

The eyes see there materials for building,
See the difficulties, too, and the obstacles.
The hand seeks tools to cut the wood,
To till the soil, and harness the power of the waters.
Then the hand seeks other hands to help,
A community of hands to help—
Thus the dream becomes not one man's dream alone,
But a community dream.
Not my dream alone, but *our* dream.
Not my world alone,
But *your world and my world*,
Belonging to all the hands who build.

A long time ago, but not too long ago,
Ships came from across the sea
Bringing Pilgrims and prayer-makers,
Adventurers and booty seekers,

Free men and indentured servants,
Slave men and slave masters, all new—
To a new world, America!

With billowing sails the galleons came
Bringing men and dreams, women and dreams.
In little bands together,
Heart reaching out to heart,
Hand reaching out to hand,
They began to build our land.
Some were free hands
Seeking a greater freedom,
Some were indentured hands
Hoping to find their freedom,
Some were slave hands
Guarding in their hearts the seed of freedom.
But the word was there always:
        FREEDOM.

Down into the earth went the plow
In the free hands and the slave hands,
In indentured hands and adventurous hands,
Turning the rich soil went the plow in many hands
That planted and harvested the food that fed
And the cotton that clothed America.
Clang against the trees went the ax in many hands
That hewed and shaped the rooftops of America.
Splash into the rivers and the seas went the boat-hulls
That moved and transported America.
Crack went the whips that drove the horses
Across the plains of America.
Free hands and slave hands,
Indentured hands, adventurous hands,

White hands and black hands
Held the plow handles,
Ax handles, hammer handles,
Launched the boats and whipped the horses
That fed and housed and moved America.
Thus together through labor,
All these hands made America.
Labor! Out of labor came the villages
And the towns that grew to cities.
Labor! Out of labor came the rowboats
And the sailboats and the steamboats,
Came the wagons, stage coaches,
Out of labor came the factories,
Came the foundries, came the railroads,
Came the marts and markets, shops and stores,
Came the mighty products moulded, manufactured,
Sold in shops, piled in warehouses,
Shipped the wide world over:
Out of labor—white hands and black hands—
Came the dream, the strength, the will,
And the way to build America.
Now it is Me here, and You there.
Now it's Manhattan, Chicago,
Seattle, New Orleans,
Boston and El Paso—
Now it is the U.S.A.

A long time ago, but not too long ago, a man said:

> ALL MEN ARE CREATED EQUAL . . .
> ENDOWED BY THEIR CREATOR
> WITH CERTAIN INALIENABLE
> RIGHTS . . .

AMONG THESE LIFE, LIBERTY
AND THE PURSUIT OF HAPPINESS.

His name was Jefferson. There were slaves then,
But in their hearts the slaves believed him, too,
And silently took for granted
That what he said was also meant for them.
It was a long time ago,
But not so long ago at that, Lincoln said:

> NO MAN IS GOOD ENOUGH
> TO GOVERN ANOTHER MAN
> WITHOUT THAT OTHER'S CONSENT.

There were slaves then, too,
But in their hearts the slaves knew
What he said must be meant for every human being—
Else it had no meaning for anyone.
Then a man said:

> BETTER TO DIE FREE,
> THAN TO LIVE SLAVES.

He was a colored man who had been a slave
But had run away to freedom.
And the slaves knew
What Frederick Douglass said was true.
With John Brown at Harpers Ferry, Negroes died.
John Brown was hung.
Before the Civil War, days were dark,
And nobody knew for sure
When freedom would triumph.
"Or if it would," thought some.

But others knew it had to triumph.
In those dark days of slavery,
Guarding in their hearts the seed of freedom,
The slaves made up a song:

>> KEEP YOUR HAND ON THE PLOW!
>> HOLD ON!

That song meant just what it said: *Hold on!*
Freedom will come!

>> KEEP YOUR HAND ON THE PLOW!
>> HOLD ON!

Out of war, it came, bloody and terrible!
But it came!
Some there were, as always,
Who doubted that the war would end right,
That the slaves would be free,
Or that the union would stand.
But now we know how it all came out.
Out of the darkest days for a people and a nation,
We know now how it came out.
There was light when the battle clouds rolled away.
There was a great wooded land,
And men united as a nation.

America is a dream.
The poet says it was promises.
The people say it *is* promises—that will come true.
The people do not always say things out loud,
Nor write them down on paper.
The people often hold

Great thoughts in their deepest hearts
And sometimes only blunderingly express them,
Haltingly and stumbling say them,
And faultily put them into practice.
The people do not always understand each other.
But there is, somewhere there,
Always the *trying* to understand,
And the *trying* to say,
"You are a man. Together we are building our land."

America!
Land created in common,
Dream nourished in common,
Keep your hand on the plow! Hold on!
If the house is not yet finished,
Don't be discouraged, builder!
If the fight is not yet won,
Don't be weary, soldier!
The plan and the pattern is here,
Woven from the beginning
Into the warp and woof of America:

ALL MEN ARE CREATED EQUAL.

NO MAN IS GOOD ENOUGH
TO GOVERN ANOTHER MAN WITHOUT
THAT OTHER'S CONSENT.

BETTER DIE FREE,
THAN LIVE SLAVES.

Who said those things? Americans!
Who owns those words? America!

Who is America? You, me!
We are America!
To the enemy who would conquer us from without,
We say, NO!
To the enemy who would divide
and conquer us from within,
We say, NO!

       FREEDOM!
           BROTHERHOOD!
               DEMOCRACY!

To all the enemies of these great words:
We say, NO!

A long time ago,
An enslaved people heading toward freedom
Made up a song:
     Keep Your Hand On The Plow! Hold On!
That plow plowed a new furrow
Across the field of history.
Into that furrow the freedom seed was dropped.
From that seed a tree grew, is growing, will ever grow.
That tree is for everybody,
For all America, for all the world.
May its branches spread and its shelter grow
Until all races and all peoples know its shade.

       KEEP YOUR HAND ON THE PLOW!
         HOLD ON!

Langston Hughes was born in Joplin, Missouri, in 1902. After graduation from high school, he spent a year in Mexico with his father, then a year studying at Columbia University. His first poem in a nationally known magazine was "The Negro Speaks of Rivers," which appeared in *Crisis* in 1921. In 1925, he was awarded the First Prize for Poetry of the magazine *Opportunity*, the winning poem being "The Weary Blues," which gave its title to his first book of poems, published in 1926. As a result of his poetry, Mr. Hughes received a scholarship at Lincoln University in Pennsylvania, where he won his B.A. in 1929. In 1943, he was awarded an honorary Litt.D. by his alma mater; he has also been awarded a Guggenheim Fellowship (1935), a Rosenwald Fellowship (1940), and an American Academy of Arts and Letters Grant (1947). From 1926 until his death in 1967, Langston Hughes devoted his time to writing and lecturing. He wrote poetry, short stories, autobiography, song lyrics, essays, humor, and plays. A cross section of his work was published in 1958 as *The Langston Hughes Reader*.

VINTAGE BIOGRAPHY AND AUTOBIOGRAPHY

VINTAGE FICTION, POETRY, AND PLAYS